Leeds Library and Information Service
24 hour renewals
http://www.leeds.gov.uk/librarycatalogue
or phone 0845 1207271
Overdue charges may apply

YESTERDAY'S COUNTRY CUSTOMS

A HISTORY OF TRADITIONAL ENGLISH FOLKLORE

HENRY BUCKTON

The
History
Press

First published 2012

The History Press
The Mill, Brimscombe Port
Stroud, Gloucestershire, GL5 2QG
www.thehistorypress.co.uk

British Library Cataloguing in Publication Data.
A catalogue record for this book is available from the British Library.

ISBN 978 0 7524 6797 9

Typesetting and origination by The History Press
Manufacturing managed by Jellyfish Print Solutions Ltd
Printed in India.

CONTENTS

ACKNOWLEDGEMENTS

I would like to thank the following individuals and organisations for their help in putting this book together:

Chapter One 'Hobby Horses' thanks to: Muriel Marrison; Phil Underwood, The Original Sailors Horse www.mineheadhobbyhorse.co.uk; Daphne McCutcheon, www.minehead-online.co.uk; and Sandy Glover.

Chapter Two 'Hunting of The Earl of Rone' thanks to: Barbara Brown, secretary of the Earl of Rone Council.

Chapter Three 'Cheese Rolling' thanks to: The *Citizen*; Paul Biggins, www.ecofocus.co.uk; Jane Harrad-Roberts Marketing Projects the Chester Food and Drink Festival; Cal Williams, www.randwick.org.uk; and Valerie Martin.

Chapter Four 'Shrovetide' thanks to: Lorna Dirveiks, secretary of The Friends of Atherstone Heritage; David Stowell; Stephen McKay; Michael Brace; and Andy Savage, www.derbyphotos.co.uk.

Chapter Five 'Unusual Sports and Games' thanks to: Richard Croft; Biff Raven-Hill, www.wartimehousewife.wordpress.com; and Steve Foster, chairman of Egremont Crab Fair and Sports, www.egremontcrabfair.com.

Chapter Six 'Mumming' thanks to: Peter J. Walls; Tom Hughes, Education Officer for Cheshire Museums; Will Riding; Pam Fray; and Colin Smith.

Chapter Seven 'Straw Bears' thanks to: James Yardley; Brian and Christine Kell; Peter Williams (Director of The Whittlesea Straw Bear Festival 2008-2011); From *Whittlesey Straw Bear* by George Frampton, Cambridgeshire Libraries Publications, 1989.

Chapter Eight 'Wassailing' thanks to: Glyn Baker.

Chapter Nine 'Flitch Trials' thanks to: Penny Hurley, Great Dunmow Museum Society; Catherine Metson; David Stone; and Peter Street, chairman of Dunmow & District Historical & Literary Society.

Chapter Ten 'Hocktide' thanks to: Dr Hugh Pihlens, Hungerford Historical Association, www.hungerfordhistorical.co.uk; Hungerford Virtual Museum www.hungerfordvirtualmuseum.co.uk; and Sylvia Breadmore, Clerk to the Town & Manor of Hungerford and Liberty of Sanden, www.townandmanor.co.uk.

Chapter Eleven 'Beating the Bounds' thanks to: Revd Grant Fellows; and Terry Warburton, MBE.

Chapter Twelve 'Tree Dressing' thanks to: Ed Scutt; Phil Knott; Rosie Evans, Arbor Tree Festival Committee; Julie Aalen, Weald and Downland Open Air Museum; Andrew Bain, vice chairman of the Bawming Committee; and Simon Garbutt.

Chapter Thirteen 'Jack in the Green' thanks to: Colin Bewes; Matthew Alexander and Roger Twitchin of Pilgrim Morris Men; Megan Taylor of Oyster Morris; Mike Riley of Mad Jack's Morris; Alan Henderson of Brentham Society; Verne Sanderson, Operations Manager Festivals, Arts, Theatres and Events, Medway Council; Lisa Caleno, Senior Media Officer, Medway Council; Simon Kelsey; Gordon Newton; Tim Funnell; and Keith Leech for quotes from his book *The Hastings Traditional Jack in the Green*, published by Hastings Borough Council in 2008.

Chapter Fourteen 'Rushbearing' thanks to: Peter Thomas; Peter Ludlam, Sowerby Bridge Rushbearing Association; Pauline Journeaux, Rochdale Online; Garry Stringfellow; and Ann Bowker.

Chapter Fifteen 'Well Dressing' thanks to: Sir Richard FitzHerbert, www.tissingtonhall.co.uk; Glyn Williams; Ann Pocklington; Mrs Pat Swatton; Mrs Rita Walsh; and Chris Simpson, secretary of the Buxton Wells Dressing Festival.

Chapter Sixteen 'Fire Festivals' thanks to: Simon Reed, www.golowan.org; Michael Brace; Jack Gritton, www.westwitton.org.uk, www.burningbartle.org.uk.

Chapter Seventeen 'Bonfire Night' thanks to: Sian Riddle, Lewes Borough Bonfire Society, www.boroughbonfiresociety.co.uk; Lewis Clarke; and Peter Trimming.

Chapter Eighteen 'Guy Fawkes Carnivals' thanks to: Dave Stokes, publicity officer to Bridgwater Guy Fawkes Carnival, www.bridgwatercarnival.org.uk; Chris Hocking, director and trustee of Bridgwater Guy Fawkes Carnival; Shelly Ford, secretary for Gorgons Carnival Club; and Phil Williams.

Finally, I would like to thank Robert McDowall, president of The Folklore Society, for writing the foreword to the book.

FOREWORD

ALL PUBLICATIONS THAT stimulate interest in English customs past and present are welcome because they stimulate the public interest in folklore. Such publications are particularly welcome when they include descriptions of customs that are still celebrated.

Yesterday's Country Customs is an enlightening and instructive collaboration by people who organise, participate in, or attend celebrations of country customs. Henry Buckton has assembled their narrative, thoughts and recollections in a thoughtfully presented, attractively illustrated book covering eighteen major country customs. A chapter is devoted to each of the eighteen customs featured in the book. The customs range from well-known traditions such as 'beating the bounds', 'Bonfire Night' and 'tree decorating' to more obscure customs such as 'Hunting the Earl of Rone' and 'flitch trials', which are now confined to a few or single location. Even within the chapters covering the more popular themes, those familiar with yesterday's country customs will find one or two accounts of customs and practices from less familiar sources. The featured customs and contributors are well documented for those who wish to pursue more detailed research on particular themes or customs.

Yesterday's Country Customs, like other publications in its genre, is an important contribution to maintaining the general public's awareness of the importance of country customs to folklore and folklore traditions in England. The book rightly confines itself to English country customs, which have different roots to those of its Celtic neighbours, where customs and traditions often reflect broader national, historical or political themes of struggle and strife.

This book works on a number of levels. It is an English tour guide to country customs. It is a singular example of how information on disparate customs from informed people and groups, who organise and participate in country customs, can be transformed into a well-constructed book. The book is instructive to those who have passing interest in customs and folklore, and to those who have a more detailed knowledge of English country customs and folklore. I commend the book to a wide readership.

Robert McDowall
President, The Folklore Society

INTRODUCTION

I N ENGLAND TODAY we enjoy a rich diversity of folk traditions, many of which can trace their beginnings back hundreds,
if not thousands of years. In fact in some ways they are a living
semblance of the nation's history. They stem from every phase of our
antiquity and embody all the peoples who have traditionally enriched
our culture, from the Celts to the Hanoverians. They encapsulate into
the nation's popular psyche some of the greatest moments from our past,
and celebrate best-loved heroes or infamous villains.

In this book we visit some of the best-known examples, which are regularly attended by thousands of people. Some of these are now regarded as
national, rather than local customs and draw supporters from around the
country and indeed throughout the globe. Few of them have a clear definition and in many cases, scholars argue as to their origins and purpose.

As well as experiencing the way in which these customs are observed
today, we look back at their histories to try and discover how and why
they might have begun, and how they have evolved over the intervening
centuries into colourful glimpses of England's past.

The book is largely written with the help of people who either run
these celebrations, or have been involved with them over the years. Its
title, *Yesterday's Country Customs*, might seem slightly contradictory, as
all of the events covered are very much alive and kicking today. However,
the majority of them are revivals that try and recreate celebrations of the
past. Nor are they only celebrated in the countryside, as some of them
take place in towns and cities. That said, when most of these customs

were first practised, even the most urban spot in the country was a small rural outpost. Collectively, these and many other similar events have contributed to the unique character of the English people and provide a tangible link to the way our ancestors both lived and celebrated.

Henry Buckton, 2012

HENRY BUCKTON IS a social historian, writer and researcher. He is the author of a number of books and also writes and presents history DVDs. He lives in Somerset.

1

HOBBY HORSES

OUR JOURNEY THROUGH some of England's quintessential folk customs begins on May Day in the Somerset coastal town of Minehead, where Exmoor sweeps down to meet the sea. Townsfolk slumbering in their beds are rudely awoken by the sound of beating drums and musicians, as a Hobby Horse makes its way to a crossroads on the edge of town. A Hobby Horse, or 'Obby 'Oss as they are pronounced in some places, will often make an appearance in other parts of the country as a character within other rituals, but in one or two locations, including Minehead, they are the central feature of their very own festival.

For some people, it has to be said, it is a particularly rude awakening, as they may not have been in bed for that long. This is because the festival actually begins on the night before May Day and some of the revellers are known to drink long into the small hours of the morning. The night before May Day is known as 'Show Night.' The festival always begins on the eve of May, unless it falls on a Sunday, in which case it is held on the Saturday. It then goes on for the next four days and, during the final night, a ceremony takes place called the Bootie.

But, like all ancient festivals, how did this custom originate and what does it all mean? The answer to this question, similar to most of the other ancient ceremonials we shall observe, is that we simply do not know. What we do know is that May Day has been celebrated as a festival in Minehead since at least 1465. The first recorded mention of the Hobby Horse comes from a ledger at Dunster Castle dated 1792, when it was invited to dance before the lord and lady of the manor and paid five shillings for its performance. Minehead is an ancient town whose lifeblood has always been the sea, where much of its trade came from South Wales on the other side of the Bristol Channel. From here commodities

In this picture showing a Sailor's Horse on the Quay at Minehead, Richard Martin is pictured with the moustache and cap to the right of the accordion player. Mr Martin, who lived in the tall house to the left of the picture, was the keeper of the Hobby Horse for many years. He was the great uncle of Muriel Marrison, who is the girl front right, with her hand on the smaller child's shoulder. The photo dates from the early 1920s. (Courtesy of Muriel Marrison)

such as coal, fish, butter, wool, sheep and cattle, would all have been ferried and unloaded in the harbour for distribution around southern England.

There are various trains of thought as to the origins of the Hobby Horse festival. One tradition claims that it dates right back to the time of the Vikings, when the Hobby Horse was regarded as a way of frightening off would-be invaders as it pranced and cavorted along the shore. Another suggests that it commemorates the wreck of a sea vessel at some juncture in the town's distant past. Another that it recalls the entry of a phantom ship into the harbour which, in true *Marie Celeste* style, had no crew or captain aboard. It has even been suggested that it was brought back from Africa by Somerset sailors, as its mask and costume bear striking similarities to those worn by dancers from various tribes in both west and east Africa. It is interesting that most of these claims associate the custom with the sea, although one conjecture attributes it to the May King, while others claim it to have a pre-Christian pedigree due to the fact that horse deities were worshipped in Celtic society, such as Epona. Even though the word 'Epona' was Gaulish for 'Great Mare', the goddess was more likely to have been the lady who sat on the horse, rather than the actual animal itself. Her role as the protector of all equestrian creatures was adapted by the Romans to be a goddess that looked after the welfare of their cavalry. But whatever its origin, the bottom line is that the visit of the Hobby Horse is supposed to bring good luck to the town, and the people of Minehead itself certainly seem to favour the assumption that the original nag fought off the rampaging Danes.

At Minehead there are in fact three Hobby Horses, each of which is accompanied by its own groups of musicians, who play side drums, accordions, or squeezeboxes. These musicians perform traditional tunes handed down through the generations. The three horses are the Original Sailors Horse, the Traditional Sailors Horse, and the Town Horse. They are shaped almost like boats, prompting some people to wonder whether at one time they were in fact intended to represent sea-faring craft, alluding to the town's early dependence on the sea, rather than simply representing horses.

These boat-shaped constructions have wooden frames that are pointed and slightly built up at either end. The top part is covered by ribbons and strips of fabric and the face of the dancer is obscured behind a mask attached to a tall, pointed hat. The bottom part of the structure is covered by a long, flowing,

This photograph, dating from the early 1920s, shows a little Hobby Horse that Richard Martin made for the children of Minehead, in the hope of inspiring them to enjoy and carry on the old tradition. Here the children are learning how to take part in the ceremony known as the Bootie. (Courtesy of Muriel Marrison)

fabric skirt, which is brightly coloured with rows of painted roundels. Attached to the horse's rear is a long rope, which is supposed to be its tail. The whole structure is then carried on the shoulders of the dancer by using straps, and as he swings and swaggers through the streets, the skirt appears to glide effortlessly above the road surface like some spectral apparition.

For the following narrative we follow the custom from the perspective of the Original Sailors Horse. On the eve of May Day the festivities commence from the quay outside the Old Ship Aground pub at around 6 p.m. The Original Sailors Horse and its retinue, wearing white peak caps, begin to wind their way through the town in search of charitable donations in aid of Mencap and the RNLI. Occasionally, during this progress, the horse might trap an unsuspecting bystander against a wall and then butt them with its prow. For young children this can be quite a terrifying sight, and even adults can feel intimidated by the antics of the rampant beast. However, it does have a gentler side, especially where women are concerned. Having suitably cornered a lady onlooker, it is known to dip its head and tickle her with a feather that protrudes from atop the mask. But what the horse is really hunting for are people who fail to give a donation. These he will single out and, after turning sharply around, the horse will attempt to lash them soundly with its rope tail. The attendants also go among the crowd to collect money and, when the party eventually reaches the Hobby Horse Inn on the esplanade, they all stop for a well-deserved drink, which usually turns into several, as the opening act of this annual celebration draws to its conclusion.

On May Day itself, the Original Sailors Horse starts at the quay at 5 a.m. then goes through the Old Town, arriving at Whitecross by 6 a.m. Legend says that a Dane was killed here in ancient times. The other Minehead horses also get to Whitecross at roughly the same time and they all dance – not fight as some sources suggest.

The Town Horse is a revival from about 1976, which is accompanied by a group of acolytes known as 'Gullivers', who are dressed similarly to itself but without the large boat-shaped frame. One local story tells how a man was killed by Gullivers early in the nineteenth century and since then the Original Sailors Horse has nothing to do with them, its representatives maintaining that they never will.

Eventually the Original Sailors Horse bows three times and then returns through the town to the quay. In the evening it processes to the nearby medieval village of Dunster, with its famous market place and castle. At the castle it performs its customary dance, a ritual dating back to at least the aforementioned ledger of 1792. It then comes back to Minehead, collecting further donations along its route.

On 2 and 3 May the celebrations are repeated as the horse party rises early to embark on another spree of merriment and mayhem. Traditionally, on 2 May, the Original Sailors Horse will visit the village of Alcombe, where the local children come out to be chased. Far from running out of steam, the festival gains momentum, with the final evening particularly noted for its boisterousness. This of course is Bootie night, when the horse starts out from the quay at around 6 p.m. and winds its way via Wellington Square and Bampton Street to a part of the town called Cher, of which Minehead resident Daphne McCutcheon explains:

> The festivities last till the third day of May and finish at the top of Cher steep in Minehead, where they perform the Bootie. This is where they grab an unsuspecting person who has not contributed a donation and hold him lengthwise in front of the horse. The horse then rises up and down above him. He is then dropped and has to scuttle off before the horse swings round and catches him with its tail.

Another annual 'Obby 'Oss festival occurs a little further along the coast in the north Cornish town of Padstow, where the festivities begin at midnight on 1 May. May Day has been celebrated at Padstow since at least the sixteenth century, although the earliest known record of its Hobby Horse dates from 1803. Again, there are two separate horses here, known as Old 'Oss and Blue Ribbon 'Oss. Before these make their appearance, the town is dressed with flowers and flags and unaccompanied singing is performed around the port, starting at the Golden Lion Inn. Each horse has a stable from which it emerges at the start of the festival and retires at the end of the proceedings.

Several of the customs we shall study are unequivocally allied to bouts of heavy drinking by those involved. Because of this they present us with some of our most vivid links to a merry England of old, when people drank to let off steam during their well-deserved and infrequent holidays. The fact that festivals often started and finished at alehouses added to the problem. But it was this very habit of drinking, or rather the rowdiness that accompanied it, that almost brought the curtain down on some of these ancient festivals, as a terrible pestilence swept through the land known as 'Temperance'. During the Victorian age, sombre leaders of Church, politics, industry and social reform, bemoaned the evils of alcohol and strived for what they termed a 'temperate society'. The two Hobby Horses at Padstow are a surviving reminder of this episode in our history. At one time there was only one horse, but in the late nineteenth century the town's Temperance movement introduced its own

Horse, as an attempt to discourage onlookers from drinking. Symbolically, the 'Old 'Oss is stabled at the Golden Lion Inn, while the Blue Ribbon 'Oss finds stabling at The Institute.

Emerging from their stables, the two Hobby Horses dance around the town, led by their own acolytes called 'Teasers' and accompanied by a procession of complimentary dancers and musicians playing drums and accordions, often numbering several dozen. The Hobby Horse costumes are far less grand than those used at Minehead and are little more than a gruesome mask attached to a tall, pointed hat, and a skirt of black shiny material that hangs down from a circular frame to about knee-height. This skirt is used to good effect to trap young maidens as they pass through the town. Protruding from the front of the frame is a small horse's head with snapping jaws made of wood, and a long flowing mane. At the other end of the horse there is a small tail made of horsehair. The hat and other accoutrements adorning 'Old 'Oss are coloured white and red, and its supporters wear red scarves to illustrate their allegiance. The Blue Ribbon 'Oss on the other hand is decorated white and blue, with its supporters following suit. During the day a number of junior or Colt 'Osses also appear in their own May Day parade, operated by children, and at some point in the late afternoon, 'Old 'Oss and Blue Ribbon 'Oss meet at the maypole to forget their historic differences and dance together.

Of course in its most basic form a hobby horse is a child's toy. Just as children today pretend to drive cars in order to emulate their parents, in olden days when most transport was by horsepower, children pretended to be adults by riding a hobby horse. For poorer children this would normally be a stick with a carved wooden head, while for the elite brood of society, these could have been quite sumptuous, with stuffed fabric heads, reins, manes, and perhaps even saddles. A deluxe model might even have had little wheels to help it along the path. This toy was also sometimes referred to as a 'cock horse' as in the nursery rhyme: 'Ride a cock horse to Banbury Cross, to see a fine lady upon a white horse.'

Banbury is a town in Oxfordshire whose crosses were famously destroyed on 26 July 1600 by Puritans, who adhered to strict religious and moral convictions. Old-fashioned customs and revelry were considered ungodly, so were definitely 'out'. There were three crosses in Banbury: The High Cross, The Bread Cross and The White Cross, and it was not until 1859 that a new cross was built in the town centre to commemorate the marriage of Princess Victoria to Prince Frederick of Prussia. Princess Victoria was the eldest daughter of Queen Victoria and Prince Albert, who went on to become a queen and empress in her own capacity. In 2000, to celebrate the 400th anniversary of the destruction of their crosses, someone had a brainwave to capitalise on the town's connection with the old nursery rhyme, and the Hobby Horse Festival was born.

Unlike at Minehead and Padstow, the Banbury festival would not simply feature a few rival horses, but dozens. In fact, the festival became a celebration of animal disguise costumes, both in England and around the world. It was a great success and has been going strong annually ever since, and is usually held over the first weekend in July. The festival now lasts for three days from Friday to Sunday, culminating in a grand civic procession through the town led by the town's mace-bearer, going from the Town Hall to the People's Park, via Banbury Cross. At the park there is an afternoon of fun and games as part of what is called Town Mayor's Sunday, which includes mass hobby horse racing.

To further capitalise on the town's association with the nursery rhyme, a bronze statue of the 'fine lady upon a white horse' was unveiled by Princess Anne in April 2005, just yards from the present Banbury Cross. It was designed by Andrew Edwards, Carl Payne and Julian Jeffery of Artcycle Ltd. Nobody really knows who the fine lady was, although her most likely identity was a

The new statue of the fine lady upon a white horse at Banbury in Oxfordshire, which was unveiled by Princess Anne in 2005. In this picture at least two of the horses were made by Eton College, originally for a theatrical event. These are the white horse far left and the black horse in the centre. (Courtesy of Sandy Glover)

member of the family that lived at nearby Broughton Castle. Today though, during every annual festival, people from all around the world will ride their cock horses to Banbury Cross, to see this fine lady upon her white horse. And they do come from all around the world, as the Banbury Hobby Horse Festival has already established itself as a focal point for followers of this ancient art.

Traditional and well-known hobby horses have been attracted to the festival since its inception. These have included Sam, a horse belonging to the Ilmington Morris Men from south Warwickshire, which is reputed to be over 100 years old. The horse is said to have been made in 1899 by a certain Edwin Hancox of Stratford-upon-Avon and was introduced into Ilmington tradition by one Sam Bennett. Then there is Hob Nob, the Salisbury civic dragon paraded by Sarum Morris; and Cobb's Horse of the Adderbury Morris Men. Even Minehead's famous creations have made appearances, first visiting in 2001.

Hooden Horses from Kent also make regular appearances. These originated from an area around Folkestone and Whitstable during the nineteenth century. A horse's head carved out of wood is affixed to the top of a four-foot pole, and then paraded out to big houses just before Christmas. They were made by carters and ploughmen, and the person carrying the pole would be hunched beneath hessian sacking. The horse's head had jaws that could snap together when a cord was pulled. At each stop a short play was performed to the gentry and their anticipated reward was either money or drink, both appreciated at a time of year when farm work was in short supply.

In Cheshire, there was a similar custom called hodening, when a real horse's skull, the jaw of which was wired to clack open and shut, was mounted on a wooden frame and carried from door to door at Christmas by a person hidden beneath a cape. And in South Yorkshire and Derbyshire, around Christmas and New Year, groups of men would perform a drama in private houses and pubs, based on an old folk song entitled 'The Old Horse', during which they would be accompanied by a hobby horse called 'Owd 'Oss. This was another real horse's skull with snapping jaw, which was painted black and red and mounted on a wooden pole also carried by a man concealed beneath a cloth. This custom was very popular in the area around Dore in the late nineteenth century and persisted until at least the 1970s.

As well as these traditional hobby horses, every year the competition is open to adults and children alike to design new costumes, which really help to give the Sunday parade a carnival atmosphere. New designs have included dragons, elephants and unicorns. Another popular addition to the festival are the floral horses instigated by the Banbury in Bloom committee. As well as the costumes, the festival now includes street theatre, morris dancing, work-shops, and the Feast of the Beasts, which is a gathering in the Town Hall on the Saturday evening where festival participants enjoy a meal and drinks, followed by a ceilidh and a chance to entertain and be entertained by their fellow creatures.

Of course no Banbury Hobby Horse Festival would be complete without an appearance by the fine lady herself, and every year since the start of the festival she has helped to lead the Sunday procession, although with the five o'clock stubble quite apparent on the face of the rider, she is distinctly more 'rough gentleman' than 'fine lady'!

2

HUNTING OF
THE EARL OF RONE

F OR HUNDREDS OF years a hobby horse has been an integral character within another strange custom that takes place annually at the village of Combe Martin on the north Devon coast, near Ilfracombe. This custom, occurring over the four days of the Spring bank holiday weekend at the end of May, is called the Hunting of the Earl of Rone. Unfortunately for the luckless earl in question, his fate never changes, as each year he meets a violent and soggy end.

The festival opens on the Friday evening in Holdstone Way, where villagers, many dressed in period costumes, assemble before scouring the streets in a vain attempt to seek out the infamous fugitive known as the Earl of Rone. The period represented in these costumes is very much open to interpretation and in recent years they have ranged from Tudor to Victorian, although many women simply wear timeless rustic shawls and bonnets, often adorned with floral crowns. The official line from the Earl of Rone Council is that there are no rules as to what people can or cannot wear, 'although trainers, jeans and back-packs get close to prohibition'.

The festival is run by a council of villagers from Combe Martin, although the citizens of other local villages, such as Berrynarbor, Trentishoe and Kentisbury, are encouraged to participate. However, if they do, they are expected to make an effort in terms of their attire and should at least attempt to wear something regarded as fitting the occasion. Any other visitors, not of local origin, are also welcome to come along and spectate.

Also hunting the earl during this elaborate mumming are the Hobby Horse, the Fool, and a troop of Grenadiers. In appearance, the Hobby Horse is a cross between those at Padstow and Minehead. It has the hooped frame reminiscent of the former and the skirt is punctuated with the brightly coloured roundels of the latter. It also wears a gruesome mask beneath a conical hat, and is armed with an instrument called a 'mapper'. This is the shaped representation of a horse's head complete with snapping jaw. It is quite likely that this instrument acquired its unusual name through a clerical error in times past, so perhaps it should have been called a 'snapper?'

The Fool is robed in a traditional white smock above leggings of coloured ribbons, topped by a be-ribboned hat, while the smartly dressed Grenadiers parade in scarlet tunics with gold facings and epaulettes. They also sport black breeches, white stockings, tall conical hats decorated with coloured ribbons, and carry muskets. The procession is also accompanied by a band of traditional musicians.

On the opening evening, once all the participants are duly gathered, they make their way down through the village as far as the Pack o'Cards Inn before ending the evening at the Castle Inn, having been unsuccessful in their quest. Here, a few welcome beverages help to soften their anticipated disappointment. The Castle Inn, coincidentally, is where the Hobby Horse is traditionally stabled, while the Pack o'Cards is worth visiting in its own right as one of England's most unusual follies. This grade II listed monument was built to resemble a deck of cards and has four floors, each representing one of the four suits in a pack. There are thirteen doors and thirteen fireplaces on each floor, reflecting the number of cards in a suit – and so it goes on.

The following morning the adults have a chance to recover, as Saturday is Children's Day and an opportunity for the young of the parish to dress up and perform their very own version of events. The junior party starts off from Combe Martin Primary School at 11 a.m. and makes its way to the beach, from where it progresses through the village, baying for the earl's blood. However, their efforts are equally fruitless, as the cunning villain of the piece successfully eludes all pursuers.

The senior party takes to the streets again on the Sunday afternoon, after assembling at the Sandaway Holiday Park on the Ilfracombe road at 1.30 p.m. From here they proceed to the beach and commence yet another sweep of the village at around 2 p.m. This time their search is more thorough, as they venture into back alleys that they might have missed on their previous sortie. Nevertheless, they still return to the Castle Inn empty handed, having failed to apprehend their quarry yet again.

The earl's inevitable capture finally takes place on the bank holiday Monday after the hunting party, led by the Grenadiers, sets off at 6 p.m. along Wood Lane bound for Lady's Wood. It is here, concealed among the foliage, that the outlaw is eventually discovered and taken into custody. He is attired in a smock frock padded out with straw, wears a monstrous black, white and red mask, and has a string of twelve hard sea biscuits hanging around his neck.

From Lady's Wood the prisoner is bundled back to the road, where the party is reunited with the Hobby Horse and Fool. He is then mounted, back to front, on a real donkey and paraded through the village towards the sea. The animal is decorated with flowers and also wears a necklace of twelve sea biscuits. Along the route the earl is frequently shot by the Grenadiers, and falls wounded from his mount. Thereupon he is revived by the Hobby Horse and Fool, remounted on the donkey, and carried ever onwards towards his fate.

As the party passes a house called Lynton Cottage, they observe a custom within the custom, for it was here that, during the celebrations of 1837, one of the participants, a Mr Lovering, fell from the steps and broke his neck. In commemoration, the modern-day procession passes the house in silence.

On reaching the Pack o' Cards the party stops to enjoy refreshments, before finally arriving at the beach just before sunset, where the earl – not having received any form of trial – is executed by firing squad. This time he is not revived and the Grenadiers throw his body unceremoniously into the surf.

It is hard not to feel a degree of pity for the tragic and, in some ways, pathetic figure, on which the people of Combe Martin unleash their disfavour. But who was the Earl of Rone and why does his semblance deserve to be treated with such brutality and with a complete lack of compassion?

Local legend claims he is Hugh O'Neill, Earl of Tyrone, who fought against the Tudor re-conquest of Ireland in the Nine Years War, during the latter part of Queen Elizabeth I's reign. In 1607, several years after James I had ascended to the throne, as a political refugee O'Neill was forced to flee the country with his family and retainers. The custom suggests that he was shipwrecked in a local bay called Raparee Cove and subsequently hid out in Lady's Wood, surviving only on the ships' biscuits he had procured from the stricken vessel that had disgorged him on to the English mainland. This explains both his shabby appearance, quite unbefitting of nobility, and his curious diet. It is interesting to note that there is no mention or involvement in the custom of any other members of his party. Do we assume, therefore, that all others perished in the treacherous waves of the Bristol Channel?

O'Neill himself, the story says, was eventually captured by a party of Grenadiers sent from Barnstaple after receiving intelligence as to his whereabouts. However, there is no actual historical evidence to prove that he floundered in North Devon at all, and in fact his party is known to have successfully reached the shores of Europe, eventually Spain, in which country he

The Earl of Rone is frequently shot from off his mount, only to be revived by the Hobby Horse and the Fool. (Courtesy of Earl of Rone Council)

Having received no trial, the Earl of Rone is executed by firing squad above Combe Martin beach. (Courtesy of Earl of Rone Council)

lived out the rest of his days. So why O'Neill should be associated with the custom is an intriguing mystery. The Earl of Rone Council offers the following explanation:

> Perhaps the locals were celebrating the defeat of a famous contemporary outlaw by a local landowner, a Chichester, who was the sovereign's Lord Deputy in Ireland at the time. Perhaps the Irish population in the village, who worked the mines, were in sympathy with O'Neill and his attempts to have Ireland ruled by the Irish. Some people think the custom is the last remnant of mediaeval May Games; others like to think that it is a pre-Christian, pagan, Green Man custom that has survived with the O'Neill legend attached to it. The Earl of Rone is seen as a scapegoat by others. People believe what they want to believe whether there is evidence or not – even those who take part have different ideas.

These are only a few of the suppositions relating to the event. Some suggest that it mimics the Stations of the Cross. The earl, similarly to Christ, is cruelly and publicly humiliated during the long, agonising journey to his execution.

So once again we are none the wiser as to the exact origin of the custom, or indeed its antiquity. The current celebrations can be traced to 1974, reviving a tradition that had been banned in 1837 due to the licentiousness and drunken behaviour of its followers. This earlier ceremony had always been performed on Ascension Day (the Thursday during the fifth week after Easter, or 'Holy Thursday' as it is also known).

There are a number of descriptions of how the custom was observed before the ban, including the following taken from *The North Devon Scenery Book* by Revd G. Tugwell, published in 1863:

> During the fortnight which preceded Ascension Day the Hobby-Horse and the Fool, in full dress, paraded the parish and levied contributions to defray the cost of the dresses and the other expenses of the show. On the morning of the day itself great numbers of people thronged in from the surrounding parishes and the whole village turned out in its Sunday garments and put on its liveliest aspect. At three o'clock in the afternoon the Grenadiers marched with all due pomp and circumstance of war to the neighbouring plantation called Lady's Wood, and after much parade of search, discover the fugitive Earl of Rone ineffectually hidden in the low brushwood. They immediately fire a volley, lay hold of their prisoner, set him on the Donkey with his face towards the animal's tail, and thus conduct him in triumph to the village. Here the Hobby-Horse and the Fool, and great numbers of the inhabitants, join in the procession.

At certain stations in the village the Grenadiers fire a volley, when the Earl falls from his Donkey apparently mortally wounded. Hereupon there is great exultation on the part of the soldiers, and excessive lamentation on the part of the Hobby-Horse and the Fool. After great exertion the latter invariably succeeds in healing the Earl of his wounds, and then the procession re-forms and marches onward once more. At every public-house there is also a stoppage for purposes of refreshment, and as there are many such houses in Combmartin [*sic*] the progress of the mummers is necessarily slow. Moreover there are further innumerable delays, caused by the perpetual efforts of the performers to levy additional contributions from the visitors who throng the street. As a general rule small sums are given readily, for in case of refusal the Fool dips the besom which he carries in the nearest gutter and plentifully besprinkles the rash recusant, and should not this hint be promptly taken the Hobby-Horse proceeds to lay hold of the victim's clothes with his 'mapper', and this detains his prisoner till the required blackmail is forthcoming. About nightfall the procession reaches the sea.

It is from descriptions such as this that the modern festival draws reference. A source from 1917 explains that at the time of the ban there were no less than nine public houses in the village. So, during the final flurry of celebrations, it was beginning to lose its historical importance, owing to the introduction of a good deal of rough horseplay and excessive drinking on the part of the participants. The final event, which took place in the year of Queen Victoria's ascension to the throne in 1837, was blighted with so much mirth and conviviality that most of the principal actors were 'done for' by the time they had left the third hostelry. Of course, it was during this sorry episode that Mr Lovering fell to his death from the steps of Lynton Cottage. This tragic event somewhat sobered the occasion and is said to have contributed towards its abandonment.

In the modern manifestation visitors once more flood to the streets of this, usually quiet, Devonshire village. Collections are still made throughout the weekend, and, once costs have been covered, any surplus money is donated to good local causes.

For those still baffled and bemused by the custom and unsatisfied with the explanations afforded for its observance, at the end of the day does it really matter that its true origins have been lost somewhere in the mists of time? After all, as the Earl of Rone Council states quite eloquently, what the Hunting of the Earl of Rone is really all about 'is Combe Martin celebrating itself'.

As a village, Combe Martin boasts a number of well-organised public events throughout the year, and the Hunting of the Earl of Rone is just one of the highlights. This catalogue also includes carnival week during the second week of August, which begins with the crowning of the carnival queen and features an impressive procession of colourful and imaginative floats of varying sizes. These include entries from local businesses and other organisations, some of which have been entering into the parade since 1911. Carnival week concludes on the Friday night with a spectacular fireworks display.

Combe Martin also has a well-known music festival which starts on a Friday in July, with live music every consecutive Friday, Saturday and Sunday for the next four weeks. And then there is the traditional Strawberry Fayre on the first Sunday in June. Combe Martin was once an important producer of strawberries. During the fayre, Cross Street is closed to traffic, while dozens of colourful stalls are erected to display a variety of homemade food and local crafts, and of course large helpings of Combe Martin strawberries and real Devon cream can be enjoyed on the day or taken home for tea.

3

CHEESE ROLLING

I N ENGLAND. THERE are several locations where cheese rolling occurs in a festival scenario. The examples mentioned here are very different from one another. The origins of some can be traced back centuries, while others are relatively modern customs. The most extreme of these, in which people hurl themselves down a treacherous slope, takes place at Cooper's Hill in Gloucestershire, while during the others competitors negotiate the rather less precipitous inclines of the village of Stilton in Cambridgeshire, the city of Chester, and the Cotswold village of Randwick.

The most popular of all these events is the Cheese Rolling and Wake that takes place annually at Cooper's Hill near Brockworth. In recent years people have descended on the site from all over the country in increasing numbers, both to take part or to spectate, as the occasion now enjoys a status of worldwide celebrity – or perhaps even notoriety. In fact, at the time of writing, the future of the event is very much hanging in the balance, due to health and safely fears.

There is no doubt that this is an ancient festival but, similar to many of the other customs we cover, it is impossible to trace its beginning to an exact moment in time. At the summit of Cooper's Hill there is evidence of an Iron-Age hill fort, so people have been living and working here for thousands of years. The Romans also occupied this Cotswold vantage point and some claim that the custom originates from their distant days. Certainly by the early 1800s the festival was recorded as being long-established, but if the ancient Britons did partake in such activity, they did so without the Double Gloucester cheese traditionally used in the event, as this semi-hard, unpasteurised delicacy only came into existence in the sixteenth century. So if the custom does

At the start of a cheese rolling downhill race on Cooper's Hill in Gloucestershire, the Master of Ceremonies raises his stick, counts: 'One to be ready! Two to be steady! Three to prepare.' The cheese is then released and the MC commands, 'and four to be off,' at which the competitors hurl themselves down the slope after it. (Courtesy of The Citizen)

pre-date the Hanoverians, we can only guess as to what was released down the hill at the time.

The modern event takes place at midday every spring bank holiday Monday. There are presently five main competitive downhill races, one of which is a ladies' race, when a 7-8lb Double Gloucester cheese is released down the hill, after a count of three by the Master of Ceremonies. On the count of 'and four to be off!' the competitors hurl themselves down the 200-yard long slope in pursuit. Basically, there is a one second delay between the release of the cheese and the charge of the competitors. The object of course is to catch the cheese, but as it picks up speeds of around 70mph (112kmp), this is a rare occurrence; the usual winner of the race is the first person to arrive at the foot of the hill, and it really doesn't matter how they do it. Their prize for achieving this is a whole Double Gloucester cheese, while for second and third place there is a small cash prize.

Cooper's Hill has a gradient in places of 1-in-2, so it is almost impossible to remain on your feet during the descent. Each year there are many minor injuries, such as broken ankles, wrists and other fractures. The winner of one of the 2008 races arrived at the base of the hill in an unconscious state, so was unaware of his victory until properly revived. A fleet of ambulances stand by to ferry the inevitable casualties to A&E. Apparently, one of the heats in 2005 was delayed due to the fact that all the ambulances were already in use, transporting the injured from the previous race.

Since the early 1800s, cheese rolling on Cooper's Hill has taken place nearly every year, following a similar format. However, during the Second World War, and indeed right up until the end of rationing in 1954, a wooden substitute was used, as an actual cheese was considered far too precious. And adhering to the dictates of modern health and safety regulations, at least twice in more recent years, the public event has been cancelled. But on both of these occasions a small ceremony has still taken place with a single cheese being rolled, in order to maintain the continuity of the tradition.

Unfortunately, at the time of writing, the official event had been cancelled for the third year running. There were a number of reasons for this, paramount among them the fact that the crowds had become too large for the venue, causing both a health and safety risk and chronic traffic congestion. Because of this, the organisers decided to limit numbers by selling tickets. They also wanted to move the festival to a date in June. Their plans faced a public backlash that caused them to feel the necessity to cancel the event. That said, there are still those who brave the slope each year – unofficially.

Another spot where you might observe the rolling of Double Gloucester cheeses, three in fact, is the village of Randwick near Stroud, also in Gloucestershire, where they are first blessed in a church service before being rotated around the building in an anticlockwise direction by local children. This is not necessarily a gentle affair and there is usually something of a scrabble between the children to get a turn to roll or even hurl the cheeses, and although they set out separately, there is intense competition between those chasing each of the three cheeses to try and catch the group who set off before them. Weather-permitting, the actual service is held outside the Church of St John the Baptist on the first Sunday in May, at 10.30 a.m. It is claimed that the act of rolling the cheeses wards off evil spirits, and therefore protects both the church and the village from harm. Afterwards, one of the truckles is cut up and distributed among the crowd in order to guarantee the line of 'Runnickers', as the local people call themselves. This might seem more pagan than Christian, but it is thought that eating the blessed cheese will ensure the fertility of the congregation and therefore secure the future of the community.

At one time this ceremony was held on May Day, and on the subject Miss E.P. Fennemore wrote in her *A History of Randwick* published in 1893:

MAY DAY – In the village of Randwick, hard by the Stroud cloth mills, at the appointed day-break three cheeses were carried upon a litter, festooned and garlanded with blossoms, down to the Churchyard, and rolled thrice mystically round the sacred building; being subsequently carried back in the same way upon the litter in triumphal procession, to be cut upon the village green, and distributed piecemeal among the bystanders.

In Miss Fennemore's account it seems that all three of the cheeses were handed out among the villagers to eat, whereas today two of them are kept until the following Saturday, when they are rolled down a steep footpath in the village called Well Leaze, during a celebration known as the Randwick Wap.

The Randwick Wap is the revival of a medieval custom which was said to be staged annually in the village at least 700 years ago. The current celebration enjoyed its fortieth anniversary in 2011. The festivities include a colourful procession of villagers wearing traditional costume accompanied by musicians, which wends its way from Randwick's war memorial to a spot called the Mayor's Pool. A mock mayor is elected for the occasion, who, along with the May Queen, is carried shoulder high along the processional route in decorated chairs. The parade is led by a mop man, who swishes a wet mop to clear the route of spectators. The mayor's entourage also includes the flag man, flag boys, a sword bearer, princesses and ladies-in-waiting for the May Queen, and bearers of the Double Gloucester cheeses. On reaching the pool, the chairs holding the mayor and May Queen are set down, and the mayor is ceremonially anointed with water from a silver salver and ladle, although a drenching from a bucket has been known on occasion. In 2011 the mayor was female, in fact only the fourth or fifth woman to hold the office in the event's current forty-year run, and being a 'more senior' village figure was treated to just the ladle-full.

In her book, Miss Fennemore quoted the following extract from *County Folk-lore*, dated May 1784, and written by an author who simply signed themself 'J.L.':

As I was last year passing through the village of Randwic [*sic*], near Stroud, in Gloucestershire, my attention was attracted by a crowd of people assembled round the horsepond, in which I observed a man, on whom I imagined the country people were doing justice in that summary way for which an English mob is so famous though I was at the same time surprised to hear them singing, as I thought a psalm, since I never knew that to be a part of the form of such judicial proceedings. I soon, however, was informed of my error and learned that it being the second Monday after Easter, the people of the parish were assembled according to an annual custom (the origin of which no one could tell me) to keep a revel. One of the parish is, it seems, on the above mentioned day elected mayor, and carried with great state, colours flying, drums beating; men, women, and children shouting; to a particular horsepond, in which his worship is placed, seated in an arm chair; a song is then given out line by line by the clerk, and sung with great gravity by the surrounding crowd. The instant it is sung, the mayor breaks the peace by throwing water in the face of his attendants. Upon this much confusion ensues; his worship's person is, however, considered as sacred, and he is generally the only man who escapes being thoroughly soused. The rest of that day, and often of the week, is devoted to riot and drunkenness. The county magistrates have endeavoured, but in vain, to put a stop to this practise. J.L.

Although in the eighteenth century none of the villagers were able to offer an explanation of the custom to the writer of this account, the legend mooted today is that the tradition originated when the church was built. The story goes that one of the workmen so enjoyed a liquid supper that his colleagues refreshed him with a visit to the pool. More serious versions link the event to priestcraft, or to a Saxon word 'Wappenshaw', which refers to a time when men gathered to show they were ready for battle.

It is interesting to note in this early account that no mention is made of cheese rolling during the Wap. Today, however, following the visit to the Mayor's Pool, the procession continues to the Well Leaze, where the two Double Gloucester cheeses kept from the previous Sunday are rolled down the steep slope three times, one by the mayor and the other by the May Queen. So perhaps somewhere in between these dates, two customs have combined into the current Wap celebration.

After the procession the event continues in the afternoon with concerts by various bands, country dancing, stalls and many other forms of entertainment, giving the whole thing the feel of a contemporary country fair with a medieval twist.

The variation of cheese rolling practised in Stilton is now equally genteel. Although the village has been associated with the famous blue cheese that bears its name for almost 300 years, the custom in its present form only began here around the middle of the twentieth century. It has now become a major event in the village calendar, taking place annually on the May Day bank holiday Monday. Villagers and visitors flock to the High Street to watch as teams compete for the honour of being proclaimed Stilton Cheese Rolling Champions.

The anomaly is, of course, that Stilton cheese is exclusively made in the counties of Leicestershire, Derbyshire and Nottinghamshire, nowhere near Cambridgeshire whatsoever. So how did the association come about? It all stems from a gentleman called Cooper Thornhill, who, during the eighteenth century, was the proprietor of the Bell Inn, in Stilton, a village strategically placed along the Great North Road, which ran between London and York. This made Stilton a convenient stopping place for stagecoaches, particularly the mail coach.

In 1730, while visiting a farm near Melton Mowbray in Leicestershire, Thornhill became aware of a blue cheese being made in the locality with a distinctive flavour. Quite possibly the farm in question was Quenby Hall in Hungarton. Having never tasted anything quite like it before, an idea hatched in his mind, and, being an astute businessman, he persuaded the makers of this cheese to grant him exclusive rights to marketing it. Thereafter, the Bell Inn soon became the distribution point for blue Stilton to London, the north of England, and the wider world beyond, as wagon loads of the stuff were delivered to his premises from the farms that manufactured it.

By the middle of the twentieth century, after the building of the A1 trunk road, the village had been effectively by-passed and forgotten by the outside world. Fewer and fewer people had cause to venture into its streets, stop overnight, or sample its hospitality in other ways.

Around this time the landlord of a local pub, who had seen a big drop in his revenue, decided to revive an ancient local custom, or so he claimed. He began to roll a Stilton cheese along the road in front of his establishment. Naturally people were curious, so they began to stand and watch, and wonder what he was doing. On explaining that it was an ancient custom, some people began to join him, until it became quite a popular pastime. As well as having the desired effect of drawing people into his pub and the village in general, a new sport was born, or perhaps even reborn if there was any element of truth in his convincing claims.

In the beginning there seems to have been very little coherence to the games that developed from this, which initially took place each Easter Monday. Somebody at some point produced a piece of wood in the shape of a Stilton cheese to replace the genuine article that had been hitherto employed. A starting line was drawn up somewhere between the Stilton Cheese Inn and the Talbot Inn, with the finishing line outside the Bell Inn. Local men formed themselves into teams and keenly tussled and spilled, as they rolled the cheese along the course, until the first team to steer it across the finishing line claimed the victory.

In today's competition, the starting point is outside the Bell Inn and the Angel Inn, with the finish line drawn at the crossroads between the bottom of

A ladies team competes for the Stilton WI Cup, during the annual cheese rolling at Stilton in Cambridgeshire. (Courtesy of www.ecofocus.co.uk)

Fen Street and Church Street. Teams consist of four members, either all male or all female, and as they roll the cheese along its route, each team member has to roll it at least once or face disqualification. The male teams vie for the Bell Cup, while the ladies roll to win the Stilton WI Cup. Both are knockout competitions with quarter finals, semis, and a grand final. There is even a competition for juniors, who compete for the Stilton Parish Council Shield.

Teams are encouraged to wear fancy dress, which, although often restricting, all helps to add a dash of colour and humour to the proceedings. And of course, there are prizes for the most original costumes.

According to the Stilton Community Association, the sport has become more genteel over the years. 'But,' they state, 'we still get the tumbles and spills as in former days. The friendly rivalry grows during the competition as each team passes through to the next round. So we end up with some very competitive finals.'

Coupled with the honour of winning the two coveted trophies, the successful male team receives prizes of a whole Stilton cheese and beer, while for the ladies the cheese is partnered by wine. But the real prize is the cherished immortality of being Stilton Cheese Rolling Champions.

The Stilton Cheese Rolling is normally officially opened by a guest celebrity. In this instance actors Robbie Coltrane and Warwick Davis have the honour. (Courtesy of www.ecofocus.co.uk)

Today, the event takes place annually on the May Day bank holiday and begins at around 10.30 a.m., with the official opening by a celebrity guest of honour. This is followed by the arrival and crowning of the May King and Queen by the previous year's royal couple. Then there is the judging of the children's fancy dress and decorated buggies, followed by maypole and country dancing, performed by children of Stilton and Holme schools, and morris dancing by adult groups.

At 12 noon the cheese-rolling teams take part in a pre-competition parade, where the best-dressed adult and junior teams are awarded prizes. The junior championships usually kick off at around 12.30 p.m., with heats for ladies and men following shortly afterwards. The day builds up to a crescendo of excitement, culminating with the adult finals at around 2.30 p.m., followed by the Champion of Champions, and the presentation of prizes and trophies.

The whole day is accompanied by other related activities, such as the funfair, ferret racing, and numerous stalls. The proceedings end in the evening with the cheese-rolling concert held on the playing fields. And, as the programme of events states, 'If you don't have fun here – you won't have it anywhere!'

Another cheese-rolling competition takes place in the city of Chester, but this particular custom is even newer than the Stilton championships. It takes place to herald the start of the city's annual Food and Drink Festival. Teams from Cheshire compete against visiting cheese rollers from Lancashire, Stilton, and other challengers.

The Chester Food and Drink Festival is held over Easter weekend. It begins when a wheel of Cheshire cheese, which has earlier been blessed by the Dean of Chester Cathedral, is carried around the old Roman city walls from the Dean's Field to Eastgate Street. It is then taken through the streets to The Cross, for the cheese rolling to commence. During this journey the cheese is accompanied by quite a procession of people. As well as the competitors, there are Roman soldiers, children from local schools, the Lord Mayor of Chester, and councillors of every description. The cheese rolling itself takes place at 11 a.m. down the cobbles of ancient Bridge Street, along which obstacles are placed for the competitors to manoeuvre around or between. The event, which is intended to emphasise the point that food and drink is one of the county's most important products, has already established itself as a firm favourite with both locals and visitors, all of whom are left grinning like Cheshire cats.

Perhaps the least-known and most unusual cheese rolling event takes place in the village of Findon near Worthing, in the South Downs of West Sussex. The reason why it is little known to anybody outside of the immediate community is because it only takes place on coronation days, and, obviously, that is not very often. I discovered its existence through Findon historian Valerie

Neil Bates of the Made in Cheshire team rolls to victory around the city obstacle course in the 2008 Chester Cheese Rolling competition. (Courtesy of Chester Food and Drink Festival)

Martin, whose own knowledge of the event, which of course was last practised in 1953 for the coronation of Queen Elizabeth II, was through a local man, the late John Pelling, himself a witness to the last event.

Mr Pelling explained that his grandmother, Marmie Ockendon, had told him of earlier events when cheeses had been rolled down Church Hill, near the village cricket pitch. It was a sport in which only ladies took part. Cheeses were rolled downhill and the women of the village chased after them. If they caught one, as his grandmother claimed to have done, they were allowed to take it home. Concerning his own memory of the more recent event, he revealed:

> I have only seen it once, in 1953. I was working at Wintons (the local shop) and Dennis Winton said to me, go down into the cellar and bring up four Red Dutch cheeses and give them to Ernie May, who was the organiser. The event along with other sports was held in the Glebe Meadow by the village hall. Women were divided into groups and held while the cheeses were rolled. They needed a good throw to get them going as the field was quite flat. I thought at the time it would have been more thrilling in the old days on Church Hill. Mrs Brotherhood and Mrs Luther each won a cheese.

I wonder if it was the potential for twisted ankles during previous events that prompted the organisers to change its location in 1953 from Church Hill to the gentler undulations offered by the Glebe Meadow? If it was, then perhaps health and safety is not such a new consideration after all?

4

SHROVETIDE

CHEESE IS NOT the only type of foodstuff to feature in its own traditional custom. One of the country's most popular food-related anniversaries occurs on Shrove Tuesday, more commonly known as Pancake Day. Each year millions of parents regimentally dish up pancakes to their children, who eagerly rush home from school with anticipation. Today you can even buy them ready-made in supermarkets. We all take this celebration for granted now as something we do without question, but how many people actually know why we eat pancakes on this particular date?

The word 'shrove' is the past tense of the English verb 'to shrive', which is a term used in the Christian faith with regards to the week before Lent, often referred to as 'Shrovetide', when believers sought to obtain absolution for their sins by way of confessing to a priest and doing penance. Shrove Tuesday was the last day before Lent, which begins on Ash Wednesday, recorded as such for at least a thousand years. The date of Shrove Tuesday is of course dependent on Easter, as it applies to the forty days leading up to Holy Week. As Easter is a moveable feast, the start of Lent can vary accordingly from 3 February to 9 March. It derived from the forty days that Jesus spent fasting in the wilderness, preparing for his ministry. Following his example, many people resolve to give things up at this time of year, such as smoking or chocolate. It is also a time when tardy Christians might attend Mass more frequently, for a while at least.

The concept of Pancake Day actually stems from this act of fasting as a means of penance, as during Lent Christians were expected to eat simpler food that would in no way induce pleasure. Things such as meat, dairy products, eggs or jams were definitely out. Devout followers would probably eat and drink little more than bread and water during this period, although it has to be admitted that freshly baked bread can be very pleasurable, no doubt causing inner turmoil among many.

On Shrove Tuesday it therefore became the custom to use up as many rich foodstuffs as possible, rather than let them go to waste during Lent. Pancakes were a great way of doing this as they could include ingredients such as sugar, milk, fat and eggs, and could be filled with assorted rich pickings. Because of this, Shrove Tuesday had a carnival air about it, with people eating, drinking and making merry before the subsequent period of abstinence kicked in.

Shrove Tuesday is certainly not unique to England. All Catholic and even some Protestant countries traditionally call the day before Ash Wednesday 'Fat Tuesday', which is effectively the same thing. This name unquestionably pre-dates England's Reformation during the reign of King Henry VIII, so it was probably known by this name even here in earlier times.

Between the fifteenth and seventeenth centuries there was a tradition in England, largely in the West Country, called Jack 'o' Lent, during which a straw effigy of a human figure was dragged around the parish on Ash Wednesday, before being stoned and generally abused. The figure would thereafter be kept until Palm Sunday, when it was ritually burnt. It is thought that Jack 'o' Lent personified Judas Iscariot to a Christian clientele, or perhaps, if a much older custom, it represented the figure of winter, whose destruction paved the way for spring. He is mentioned by Shakespeare in *The Merry Wives of Windsor*, but the custom is now so long forgotten that it is impossible to even hazard a guess as it to origins, even though it is thought to have survived in parts of Cornwall until the nineteenth century.

Also in Cornwall was a custom called Nickanan Night, or sometimes Roguery Night, when, on the Monday before Shrove Tuesday, groups of youths would play practical jokes on their neighbours, or even carry out minor acts of vandalism. The name is thought to derive from 'Nick Nack', the name given to the practice of door knocking before running away. Having done the deed the youngsters would watch from afar and, if nobody answered the door, they would return to the property, remove something such as a potted plant, and then place it in an inappropriate location somewhere else in the village.

Shrovetide celebrations also manifested in many other ways, for instance in much of England it became a day associated with sport, when traditional football became a popular addition to the proceedings, dating back to at least the twelfth century. Legend prevails that this unruly precursor to the beautiful game started when a group of Anglo-Saxon warriors had a kick about with the head of a defeated Dane.

Traditional football was far different to the matches we admire today, with very few rules and no limit on the number of players. In fact, it was more akin to rugby than anything you might see in the Premiership. Contests were known to be energetic, often extremely dangerous for those taking part, and destructive to people's property. Because of this the government of the day did its utmost to curtail the practice, so with the passing of the Highways Act of 1835, football was banned from being played on public roads. Inevitably, the sport had all but died out by the end of the nineteenth century, although a number of places have maintained the tradition in some form.

One place where the game does survive is Atherstone in Warwickshire, where it is called the Ball Game and said to originate from the reign of King John (1199-1216). Its origin is thought to have been a match of gold played on Shrove Tuesday between lads from Warwickshire and Leicestershire, mentioned in the writings of Ralph Thompson in 1790, in which he stated, 'the Warwickshire lads won the Gold'. Today's match is a free-for-all in which anyone can take part at their own risk, as hundreds frequently do.

On the afternoon of the event shops are boarded up, local schools are closed early, residents park their cars as far away from the relevant area as possible, and

The Ball Game at Atherstone in Warwickshire, seen here in 1948, is said to have taken place each Shrove Tuesday for over 800 years. (Courtesy of the Friends of Atherstone Heritage)

traffic is diverted. Those wishing to take part and spectators alike gather in the town's main thoroughfare, which is actually a section of the old Roman road known as Watling Street. Kick-off is at 3 p.m., when the ball is thrown from a first-floor window of Barclays Bank, usually by a local sporting personality or other dignitary. The ball is specially made each year out of thick leather, making it rather too heavy to kick very far. It is decorated with ribbons and the first aim of the players is to proudly attain one of these during the struggle. The ball is then kicked up and down Long Street for the next two hours. There are no teams and no goals, and after around ninety minutes a massive scrum forms. Whoever is left clutching the ball at 5 p.m. is declared the winner and has the honour of keeping it. Lorna Dirveiks, secretary of the Friends of Atherstone Heritage, provides the following:

> The rules have changed very little over the years. The ball is thrown to the crowd at 3 p.m. and the winner is the person holding the ball at 5 p.m., the prize being the ball! Family possession of a ball is taken very seriously in Atherstone with families working as a team for the honour of winning the game. For many years the ball was thrown out by whoever was starring at the Coventry Hippodrome, but that connection ceased when the Hippodrome turned over to Bingo. Nowadays the committee chooses the celebrity and the ball is thrown out of a window at Barclays Bank. George Formby, Tommy Lawton and Larry Grayson all threw out the ball but the incident that many people remember was in 1970, when a balcony made of scaffolding poles dropped a foot or two as Ken Dodd was officiating, forcing the comedian to scramble back through the window with great agility.
>
> Until the 1970s the pitch included the whole of the town with the ball often ending up in the canal, but a limit was put on the play and the game is now strictly confined to Long Street. In 1975 the ball was smuggled away by car and held to ransom through the local paper 'The Trib'. Other times a substitute ball has had to be provided when the ball has been smuggled.
>
> In 1986 the game got out of hand in its final hour and a public meeting was called to decide the future of the game. Many would have been happy to see an end to the tradition but a committee was formed to run the game. The police had traditionally acted as referee but from 1986 the game has been in the hands of specially selected stewards helped by a police presence.
>
> In 2001 the threat was from Foot and Mouth disease. The decision to allow the game to continue only came at the eleventh hour. Ashbourne's game had to be cancelled because their game starts in the street but then goes onto the fields, so it had to stop leaving Atherstone to hog the television time.

At Ashbourne, in Derbyshire, you will find another version of the sport, which is called the Royal Shrovetide Football Match. This occurs annually on both Shrove Tuesday and Ash Wednesday. It kicks off on each occasion at 2 p.m. and could potentially finish as late as 10 p.m.

The earliest record of the game comes from the mid-eighteenth century, although without doubt it was being played long before that time, but a fire at the organising committee's office in the 1890s destroyed earlier evidence. A variation on the head story suggests that the original game played here was started when a severed bonce was tossed into the crowd, following an execution in the town during medieval times.

The royal prefix comes from 1928, when the match was turned-up by the then Prince of Wales, later King Edward VIII. The 'turner-up' in football parlance is the person who starts the day's game. On this occasion the prince got a little too close to the action and, reputedly, went home with a bloody nose. Determined not to repeat this unfortunate mishap, when Prince Charles set things in motion in 2003, he threw the ball into play from the top of a raised podium.

The game is played through the town with no limit on the number of players or restrictions on where it can be played, with the exception of cemeteries,

The ball is 'turned up' by Anthony Kent, Director of the hauliers AK Transport, during the 2005 Royal Shrovetide Football Match at Ashbourne in Derbyshire. (Photograph by Andy Savage of www.derbyphotos.co.uk)

churchyards and memorial gardens, which are strictly out of bounds. There are two teams known as the Up'ards and the Down'ards. The Up'ards are those born on the north side of the River Henmore, a brook which meanders through the town, while the Down'ards are those born to the south. Many native Ashbournians who have moved away return to play for their respective team. The starting point for each game is at a place called Shaw Croft, which at one time was an ancient meadow, but now forms the town's main car park. Each game is started from a special plinth from where the ball is thrown to the players by an invited dignitary. Before this, however, the waiting crowd sings 'Auld Lang Syne' followed by 'God Save the Queen'.

There are two goal posts in the form of small mill stones mounted on purpose-built structures 3 miles apart along the river bank. These are situated on the sites of two former mills, Sturston Mill, where the Up'ards attempt to score, and Clifton Mill, where the Down'ards score. These scoring posts were erected in 1996, replacing original mill stones that had once furnished the two buildings. The way they are now placed requires the scorer to actually be in the water to be able to claim a goal.

The new Clifton goal on the banks of the River Henmore, where the Down'ards score during the annual Royal Shrovetide Football Match at Ashbourne in Derbyshire. (Courtesy of David Stowell)

In order to score a goal the same player has to hit the ball three successive times against the mill stone. The identity of the scorer will not be known at the start of the game and will only be decided upon along the way. When the ball is eventually goaled, the game is over. If this happens before 5 p.m., a new ball is released from the Shaw Croft podium and another game started. If, however, a goal is scored after 5 p.m., play ends for the day. If there is still no score by 10 p.m., the contest stops automatically. During the game itself the ball can be kicked, carried or thrown, although it generally moves along in a series of giant scrums involving dozens, if not hundreds of people, which are known as 'hugs'.

The balls themselves are bigger than ordinary footballs and are filled with cork, which enable them to float in the river. Each is hand-painted by local craftsmen. As a usual rule, the first ball to be turned-up has a design which somehow relates to the dignitary who has been invited to set it into play. If this ball is eventually goaled, it is taken away and repainted with the name and, in a design befitting the scorer, it will then be presented back to them and is theirs to cherish. If the ball is not goaled it will be similarly repainted in the design of the dignitary that turned it up and given back to them as a keepsake. In the period leading up to these matches, you will find some of the balls on display in the local pubs. Traditionally, the pubs have allegiance to one or other of the two teams.

In the Green Man Royal Hotel, visitors will see a series of wooden plaques containing a roll of honour, which lists all those who have both turned-up and those who have scored goals since 1891. It is interesting to note from this list that the event has only been cancelled twice in that time, in 1968 and 2001, both occasions due to outbreaks of Foot and Mouth disease. The game was even continued during both world wars, and indeed it is claimed that a contest was held in the trenches of the First World War between members of the local army regiment.

Another traditional Shrove Tuesday Football Match, known as the Ball Game, takes place in Sedgefield in County Durham. The custom here was for the parish clerk to provide a ball each Shrove Tuesday, which would be thrown into a gathered crowd at the market place. Those playing the game were traditionally either tradesmen or countrymen from the town and neighbourhood, although this isn't necessarily the case today.

At 1 p.m., an invited guest will pass the ball through a bull ring on the village green three times, before it is thrown to the crowd, who wait patiently for the completion of this ancient ritual, which is possibly 1,000 years old. The ball is then kicked, thrown and chased in another free-for-all deserving of the often-mooted title of 'Mob Football'.

The object of the melee which follows is to 'alley the ball', meaning to score a goal. The goal itself is a stream at the south of the village. However, the ball cannot be alleyed before 4 p.m., so in the meantime it is played around the town and surrounding villages, usually ending up at each pub along the route at some point. In fact, the incentive for the players is that the first person to get the ball to each pub usually receives a free drink. After the ball has been alleyed at the river, it is finally returned to the bull ring and passed through it again to end the game.

Another Shrove Tuesday Football match is played at Alnwick in Northumberland, which is known as Scoring the Hales. A 'hale' is the local term for a goal. Today, it is played in a large meadow called The Pasture, although in earlier times it was actually contested both there and through the streets of the town, a custom dating back to 1762. However, this caused so much devastation and outrage by the town's inhabitants that in 1822 magistrates enforced the Alnwick Improvement Act, which banned all street games including football, bull baiting, cock throwing and bonfires. In 1825 it was confined to the meadow alone thanks to the Duke of Northumberland, who, until then, had always paid for the damage to people's property. Legend here claims that the original ball was yet another severed head, in this instance that of a Scotsman.

Any readers thinking that the reference to cock throwing in the last paragraph is a mistake and should have been 'cock fighting', will be intrigued to learn that cock throwing really did exist. It was also sometimes known as 'cock-shying' or 'throwing at cocks'. This was a blood sport widely practised in England until the late eighteenth century, in which a cockerel would be trussed to a post while people took turns to throw special weighted sticks at it called 'coksteles'. This basically went on until the bird had been killed. Cock throwing was traditionally associated with Shrove Tuesday and was thought to symbolise the traditional enmity the English held towards the French at the time – the cockerel was said to represent a Frenchman.

The games played at Alnwick in the years before moving entirely to The Pasture were started by the ball being thrown to the assembled crowd from the barbican of Alnwick Castle, traditionally by the Duke of Northumberland himself. A similar thing still applies today, except the ball is now thrown down to the chairman of the Shrovetide Football Committee, who waits below to catch it. However, instead of kicking the ball immediately, as in former times, it is now ceremonially carried from the castle walls, across the River Aln, and onto the field of play, preceded by the duke's piper.

There are two teams, one representing the parish of St Michael, the other the parish of St Paul. There are normally around 150 players on each side.

The goals are decked with foliage and stand roughly 400 yards apart. Kick-off is at 2 p.m. and the object of the game is to score hales. Once a hale has been scored the teams change ends. The first team to score two hales are the winners, after which the ball is carried back to the river and thrown in. Whoever manages to get it out at the other side is allowed to keep it, but in order to do so they will first have to swim the Aln.

Another ancient football match takes place at Corfe Castle in Dorset, which is known as the Shrove Tuesday Football Ceremony of the Purbeck Marblers, and has been in existence for many hundreds of years. On this annual anniversary Freemen of the Company of Marblers and Stone Cutters of Purbeck gather at the Fox Inn, along West Street. At 12 noon they move across to the Town Hall to hold their annual meeting and to introduce new apprentices into the Order. From the Fox, successful applicants are subsequently summoned to the Town Hall, themselves clutching a quart of beer and a penny loaf to pay their dues, and are welcomed as Freemen of the Order.

On the conclusion of all their business, those present have a kick about with a football at 1.30 p.m. The game takes them around the parish boundary and back to the Town Hall. At one time a pig's bladder was used for this purpose. Little notice is paid to traffic during their progress, although it has to be said that the current event is decidedly more civilised than in previous times. In 1992, the match came to an abrupt end when a young policeman on secondment from the north of England and ignorant of the tradition, confiscated the ball.

In Cornwall there is a sport known as Cornish Hurling, or Hurling the Silver Ball, which is played in the town of St Columb Major, near Newquay, on Shrove Tuesday, and then again on the Saturday eleven days later. This was once very common throughout the county but now only survives in one or two places. In fact, many regard it as Cornwall's national sport, along with Cornish wrestling. It is of Celtic origin and thought to celebrate the lengthening of the days at this time of year, so technically has nothing to do with Lent. There is a similar game in Ireland, which allows the use of sticks. The ball is the size of a cricket ball and is made from apple wood and covered with silver.

Thousands of people flock to the town each year to experience this glimpse of the past, which starts with a throw up in the market square. Local men then proceed to pass and throw the ball to each other as the game progresses through the streets, which remain open to the traffic. There are two teams comprising either townsmen or countrymen. The game generally disrespects private property as it barges its way through gardens and yards. Strangely, the object of the game is to score an own goal. The countrymen score at a granite trough in a nearby field, while the townsmen aim for an ancient Celtic cross. The game can also be won by taking the ball across the parish boundary. Another version of the game is played in St Ives on the first Monday after 3 February, and celebrates the anniversary of the consecration of the parish church in 1434.

One of Cornwall's most famous ancient monuments are the stone circles near Minions, known as The Hurlers. These are thought to be the remains of men turned to stone as a punishment for hurling on a Sunday.

The village sign at Olney in Buckinghamshire, where the very first pancake race is claimed to have taken place. (Courtesy of Stephen McKay)

Shrove Tuesday was once enjoyed as a half holiday in England, which began at 11 a.m. with the sounding of a church bell, and there are still one or two places where a vestige of this survives. At Scarborough, for instance, the foreshore is closed to all traffic, schools finish early, and everybody is invited to skip by the ringing of the pancake bell by the town crier. Since 1927 this has been known as the Scarborough Skipping Festival. The tradition of closing the foreshore goes back as far as the 1850s, when the occasion was known as Ball Day. Whether skipping was involved in the early days is not known, when possibly the day was more about stalls selling different foods and other novelties, but certainly by the turn of the twentieth century skipping had become an important part of the event. Traditionally, old ropes were used that had been sorted out by local fishermen and given to the children to play with.

Other harbours were also known to have held skipping events, but not necessarily on Shrove Tuesday. And the children of the hamlet of Whitechapel in Lancashire keep alive the tradition of visiting local households and asking 'please a pancake', to be rewarded with oranges or sweets. This tradition arose when farm workers took advantage of the half-day holiday to visit the wealthier farms and manors to ask for pancakes or pancake fillings, as they themselves would not have had the luxury of excess goodies to get rid of for Lent.

But perhaps the activity that most of us associate with Shrove Tuesday, other than the actual eating of pancakes, is of course pancake racing, which many of us have no doubt taken part in at school. This is said to originate from the market town of Olney in Buckinghamshire. The tradition here states that on Shrove Tuesday in 1445, a housewife of the town was so busy cooking pancakes in anticipation for the beginning of Lent, that she forgot all about the shriving church service that everyone was expected to attend. Suddenly the Shriving Bell rang out, announcing the start of the service. On hearing the bell the woman ran to the church as fast as she could, still in her apron and headscarf, and still holding a frying pan containing its pancake.

The women of Olney recreate this race every Shrove Tuesday at 11.55 a.m., and have reputedly done so every year since 1445. To take part you must have lived in the town for at least six months. The race is run from the Market Place to the Church of St Peter and St Paul. The women must toss their pancake once at the start of the race outside the Bull Inn, and again at the finish by the church, with the traditional prize being a kiss from the verger.

5

UNUSUAL SPORTS
AND GAMES

AROUND THE COUNTRY there are a number of other customs that are descended from ancient games, some of which are similar to Shrovetide Football although held at other times of the year, while others are markedly different. Occurring on the twelfth day of Christmas, for instance, is the Haxey Hood Game, which erupts on to the streets of the north Lincolnshire village of Haxey on the afternoon of 6 January, unless the twelfth day falls on a Sunday, in which case it moves back to the 5th instead. This is not dissimilar to Shrovetide Football, during which a kind of huge rugby scrum known as the 'Sway' pushes a leather tube called the 'Hood' to one of four pubs situated in either Haxey itself or the neighbouring village of Westwoodside, where it will remain until New Year's Eve, when it will be collected in time for the next contest.

This custom, which has little or nothing to do with the religious festival sharing the same date, is said to originate from the fourteenth century, when the wife of a local landowner from the Isle of Axholme, in which these communities nestle, was riding between the two villages in question, when her extravagant silk riding hood was carried away by the breeze. The lady was the spouse of John de Mowbray, the 3rd Baron Mowbray of Axholme (1310-1361).

Thirteen peasants working nearby on their strips of land attempted to retrieve the garment by chasing it around the fields, twisting this way and that as it led them a merry dance in its bid to escape. However, the lad who did eventually trap the windswept millinery was too shy to return it to its gentrified owner, and begged one of the others to oblige in his stead.

The Lord and Chief Boggin dressed in their hunting jackets and decorated hats during the Haxey Hood Game. (Courtesy of Richard Croft)

Her ladyship enjoyed the spectacle so much that she persuaded the baron to provide thirteen strips of land so that the chase could be re-enacted annually for her amusement. This dates the game to roughly 1359, when the Baron is known to have enacted a deed granting land to commoners.

For his chivalry, Lady de Mowbray dubbed the man who had returned the hood 'a Lord', while his timid colleague she labelled 'a Fool'. The Haxey Hood Game has been played ever since and most certainly ranks among the oldest surviving traditions in the land. As a point of interest, the discerning eye can still see the evidence of ancient strip farming in the area around Haxey.

At 12 noon on the afternoon of the game, all work around the parish, from Westwoodside to the hamlets of High Burnham, Low Burnham, Eastlound and Graiselound, shudders to a grinding halt as people descend on Haxey village to either watch or participate in their time-honoured sport.

There are thirteen game officials who represent characters from the original legend, these being the Lord, the Fool and eleven Boggins, one of which is appointed Chief Boggin. Apparently they are called this because, during the original chase, each time the hood changed hands Lady de Mowbray shrieked with delight, 'It's boggined again', whatever that meant! Each character has a traditional outfit to wear. The Boggins, for instance, put on red jumpers, all except for the Chief Boggin that is, who, in similar style to the Lord, sports a red hunting jacket beneath a top hat decorated with badges and flowers. The Lord also carries a wand of office, which is a staff comprising thirteen willow wands, one of which will be upside down through the centre. These are bound together thirteen times with willow twigs, and a red ribbon sets it off. Some accounts maintain that this staff represents the sword that was used to slaughter a bullock when, in earlier times, the game was played using the animal's head. The red ribbon alludes to the creature's blood. However, there is certainly no substantive evidence to argue that this was ever actually the case.

The Fool is attired like a harlequin, with multi-coloured strips of material attached to his clothing. On his head he sports a feathered hat decorated with flowers and rags, and his face is painted with red ochre and soot. He carries a whip and a sock filled with bran, with which he belabours anyone who comes within reach.

At around 12.30 p.m. the game officials begin a crawl of the four alehouses involved with the tradition. These are the Carpenter's Arms at Westwoodside, and the Duke William Motel, the Loco, and the King's Arms, all in Haxey. At each they enjoy free drinks provided by the landlord, in the hope that this generosity will shower good luck on their own establishment and return the Hood to it once more.

This tour begins at the Carpenter's Arms, where quite a crowd gathers to sing traditional folk songs and follow the action. It is also here that the Fool has his face ceremoniously painted. The party next visits the King's Arms and, from there, steadily moves towards the parish church via both the Loco and the Duke William.

At around 2.30 p.m. the gathering eventually spills out of the final hostelry and heads towards the church led by the Fool, who, according to the ancient custom, has the right to kiss any woman encountered during his progress. On the green, before St Nicholas' Church, the Fool stands on an old mounting block known as the Mowbray Stone and delivers his traditional speech. As the church dates from between the twelfth and thirteenth centuries, its impressive tower has no doubt stood over every Hood Game that has taken place here since the custom began.

During the Fool's speech a fire is lit behind him using damp straw. This is known as 'Smoking the Fool' and at one time was quite a dangerous part of the proceedings. Hundreds of years ago, the fire was on a much larger scale and was lit beneath a tree. The Fool was then suspended from a branch of the tree by his ankles and swung back and forth until he was almost suffocated. And if that was not bad enough, he would then be cut down and dropped into the fire,

The Fool makes his traditional speech during the annual Haxey Hood Game, clutching The Hood. Smoke can be seen rising around him in a practise known as 'Smoking the Fool.' (Courtesy of Richard Croft)

scuttling away as best he could. Why anybody should have volunteered to play the Fool under such circumstances is questionable, unless of course he literally was the village fool and craved the momentary importance. However, by the start of the twentieth century common sense had prevailed and this part of the affair had been abandoned and replaced by the rather more genteel smoking which occurs today.

The Fool's speech always ends with the traditional words that the crowd chants along with: 'Hoose agen hoose, toon agen toon, if a man meets a man knock 'im doon, but doan't 'ot 'im'. This roughly translates as: 'House against house, town against town, if a man meets a man, knock him down but don't hurt him.' The towns referred to in this ditty are the villages of Westwoodside and Haxey, the houses being the four pubs.

By now a large crowd has gathered ready to play the games, which kick off at 3 p.m. from a field in Haxey. From his stone before the church, the Fool leads the crowd up the hill to the field, but before the start of the main event there is a series of prequels played mainly by younger members of the crowd. During these, twelve Hoods made of hessian sacking, which have been rolled and sewn up to prevent falling apart, are thrown to the players by the Lord. The juvenile contingent rushes forward to try and grab each in turn and get them off the field of play. If someone is tackled, they have to immediately throw the Hood into the air, unless their challenger is a Boggin, in which case the Hood is 'boggined' and has to be returned to the Lord to start it off again. The Boggins will stop the first two or three of these Hoods from leaving the field, but after a while will allow them to slip through. Anyone who does manage to get one off the field can return it later for a cash reward.

This warm up of the crowd goes on for a short while, until everybody is at fever pitch and the real Hood is launched into the crowd, which surges forward like a torrent. The Sway immediately locks in as people attempt to coerce the object towards their own favourite watering hole, by pushing and pulling. There are no teams as such and, although it is played mainly by locals, visitors are also welcome to join in. If you do decide to take the plunge, the only requirement is to help push the Hood towards your adopted alehouse.

The rules are very basic, the Hood cannot be thrown or run with, only pushed or 'Swayed' in game terminology. The Lord is also the referee and it is his responsibility to see that the game is played fairly. However, in a Sway often numbering 200 players or more, and a crowd of roughly 1,000, it is not always easy to see everything that is going on, so he also has to rely on the Boggins to help marshal the event.

Because there are no organised teams as such, the Sway can make very slow progress as it snakes from side to side. It often collapses and has to be stopped so that bodies can be pulled out from under a heap of humanity. As with the Shrovetide football matches studied earlier, health and safety is a prime concern, so the whole thing is closely supervised by the Boggins.

As can be imagined, the Sway can be extremely strong and powerful and will give no quarter to anything that stands in its path, so another job for the Boggins is to try and steer it away from causing any serious damage to people's property, although hedges and walls have been known to fall by the wayside. One of the most serious occurrences was in 2002, when two drivers for some reason decided to park near the Duke William. These cars suddenly found themselves directly in the path of the Sway, which pushed one of the vehicles 10 feet down the road, smashing it straight into the second. Nobody in their right mind would normally park their cars in the village on Hood day.

There is no time limit attached to the game as such, but they usually last a couple of hours, although they have been known to meander long into the night. The game is over once the Hood has been driven to one of the four pubs and has been touched by the landlord from his front step. The landlord in question thereafter takes charge of it for the year ahead, and is supposed to give everyone a free drink. Although with 200 or more thirsts to quench I doubt this magnanimity stretches far.

The landlord of the winning pub will pour beer over the Hood and then hang it behind the bar on two hooks, each of the four establishments having similar arrangements for when it is their turn. According to legend, after being doused in ale, the Hood used to be roasted on a spit over the pub fire and the ale drunk by those present. This may once again allude to the time when the game was reputed to have been played with a bullock's head.

Every year in the days leading up to the event the Fool and the Boggins visit villages close by to collect money for charity. In former times this was gathered to help fund the event itself. As they proceed they sing traditional folk songs such as 'John Barleycorn' and 'The Farmer's Boy!' They also wear their full game costumes, with the exception that the Fool's face is unpainted.

A not dissimilar custom is the Hare Pie Scramble and Bottle Kicking that takes place at the village of Hallaton in Leicestershire every Easter Monday, records of which date back to the eighteenth century, although it is unquestionably much older than that. Some people suggest, admittedly perhaps tongue in cheek, that the custom goes right back to pagan times when hares were reputedly sacrificed to the goddess Eostre. Of course there is absolutely no evidence in support of this but if such a goddess was ever venerated in England, you can see why some people might believe it, as the word 'Easter' may actually derive from her name.

Eostre, sometimes spelt Eastre, was said to be an Anglo-Saxon deity of the dawn, originating in Germany, so perhaps the Hare Pie Scramble was the remnant of some Easter-time ritual from pre-Christian society. Having said that, the first known mention of the goddess comes from *De Temporum Ratione* (The Reckoning of Time) (725) by the eighth-century monk the Venerable Bede (673-735), in which he attests that 'Eostur-monath' was the pagan equivalent of the month of April and that feasts in honour of the goddess had died out by his own time. But with every claim there are counterclaims, in this instance that Eostre was an invention of Bede's own making, rather than a genuine observation he had made based on historical research.

The legend behind the event is that at some point in Hallaton's distant past two wealthy ladies from the village were out walking when they were charged by a raging bull. As the beast drew down on them and their fates seemed almost sealed, a startled hare ran across the bull's path, distracting him away from the terrified women. The two ladies were convinced that God had intervened to save them, so, as an offering of thanks, they donated some land to the parish church, with the instruction to the rector that every Easter Monday he was to provide a sermon and service and arrange for two hare pies to be delivered to the poor, along with two dozen penny loaves and a quantity of ale. The ancient field name 'Hare Crop Leys' may lie at the heart of this legend, and hares are still abundant in the fields around the village.

The execution of this kindly gesture may not have gone quite according to their wishes, as it appears to have become customary for the villagers to fight each other for a share of this food and drink. Then, at some stage, the residents of the neighbouring village of Medbourne heard about the freebies and contrived to try and steal them, particularly the beer. The good folk of Hallaton were so incensed by this that they closed ranks to fight them off and reclaim what was rightfully theirs. Thus the scene was set for an unruly annual contest between the two villages that continues to this day. But just how old the legend is and whether the original deity to whom the ladies felt indebted was pagan or Christian, is anybody's guess. In 1790, the vicar of the day was so convinced that the celebration was un-Christian, that he set out to have it stopped. However, he was forced to relent after the words 'No pie, no parson' appeared on the wall of the vicarage overnight.

As its name indicates, there are two elements to this custom, the Hare Pie Scramble and the Bottle Kicking. The event begins with a parade through the villages of Medbourne and Hallaton, during which two local girls carry a large hare pie, while local men carry three small kegs, which, for the purpose of the custom, are known as 'bottles'. Two of these are full of beer, while the third, which is known as 'the dummy', is for some reason made of solid wood and is painted red and white. At the head of this procession is a man dressed in medieval costume who carries a pole surmounted by a leaping bronze hare, and a woman also in old English attire who carries a basket full of penny loaves. The parade is also accompanied by a local band.

After a church service the pie is presented to the rector at the gates of the church, to bless before its distribution. The procession then collects the decorated bottles and proceeds from the Fox Inn to Hare Pie Hill, where, at a spot called Hare Pie Bank, it is divided up and thrown to the crowd in order to honour the scramble part of the tradition. Whether those who manage to grab a slice actually eat it or not is entirely up to them, but the local dogs certainly appreciate the opportunity. The penny loaves are likewise pulled apart and thrown to the baying mob. It is interesting to note that although the first record of the event comes from a letter dated 1796, Hare Pie Bank is mentioned as far back as 1698 in lists of land owned by St Michael and All Angels' Church.

The leaping bronze hare at the top of the staff at the annual Hare Pie Scramble at Hallaton in Leicestershire. (Courtesy of Biff Raven-Hill, www.wartimehousewife.wordpress.com)

The bottle-kicking contest itself is played between two teams, one exclusively made up of citizens from Hallaton, and the other which anybody can join, representing Medbourne. Like Shrovetide football or the Haxey Hood Game, it is a rough and tumble tournament during which each team tries to get a bottle across one of two boundary streams near their respective villages, which are 1 mile (1.6km) apart.

It is a best-of-three contest and each game begins when a bottle is tossed three times in the air and, on the third time of landing, the sport commences. The Hallaton team try to force the bottles down the hill and over Hallaton Brook, near the Bewicke Arms public house, while the Medbourne side attempt to scrum the kegs over the fields towards their own village and across their own goal stream.

It is a very physical test with precious little kicking involved, let's face it, you'd probably break a toe if you tried to kick a solid block of wood. But there is a lot of pushing, shoving and scrum-like action, making the game more like rugby than anything else. In fact, the barrels used are roughly the size of a rugby ball and, one could argue, slightly shaped like one as well.

There are very few rules except for no gouging of eyes, strangling, or use of weapons. Other than that, pretty much anything is acceptable, as competitors

The three bottles are held aloft prior to the start of Hallaton's Bottle Kicking contest. Interestingly, a ball from Ashbourne's Royal Shrovetide Football Match can also be seen. (Courtesy of Biff Raven-Hill, www.wartimehousewife.wordpress.com)

grapple each bottle towards and over their goal streams. Having said that, there are no officials to actually enforce the rules anyway. Along the way the players encounter obstacles such as barbed-wire fences, hedges and ditches, but treat them with utter contempt. As a result broken bones and badly bruised bodies are not uncommon, and the local emergency services place themselves on standby.

When all three games are over the players and spectators descend on Hallaton village green, where the winners, particularly anyone who had put in notable performances, climb to the top of a 10ft-tall conical structure called the Buttercross, where the opened barrels are passed up to them to drink from before they are passed around the crowd. Finally, everyone retires to the pub for a few well-deserved pints.

Fun and games are also to be had at the Egremont Crab Fair and Sports, which is one of the oldest surviving traditional country fairs in England and certainly a throwback to how rural people entertained themselves in medieval times. This old market town sits at the foot of Uldale Valley and Dent Fell in Cumbria, on the western fringe of the Lake District National Park, and its general layout is claimed to be very similar to how it was first planned by Richard de Lucy around 1200, with a wide main street around the market place. Richard de Lucy was the local lord who resided at Egremont Castle.

The very first Crab Fair was held in 1267 and it is believed to have been staged continuously ever since, with the exception of the war years. Although the town is near the coast, the crabs in question are not of the aquatic type but crab apples. At the time, Thomas de Multon (1247-1294) was the Baron of Egremont and he was granted a Royal Charter by King Henry III to hold a weekly market each Wednesday and an annual fair, during which he would provide a cartload of crab apples to be distributed among the poor. Originally, the Crab Fair lasted for three days, 7, 8 and 9 September, which, according to the charter now kept at the British Museum, are the three days 'enduring the eve, the day of, and the morrow after the Nativity of St Mary the Virgin.'

The original fair not only coincided with this religious festival but also the end of harvesting, a time when peasants would traditionally have supplied crab apples and other wild fruits as part of their dues to the local lord. It was also a time when farming folk would undoubtedly have gathered in numbers to celebrate the end of their hard labours, and in doing so they would have enjoyed drinking and taking part in a series of rudimentary sports. So, in a way, Thomas de Multon capitalised on this seasonal occurrence and no doubt considered that he was giving something back to the community.

With the introduction of the Gregorian Calendar into Britain in 1752, the dates of the Crab Fair changed to 18, 19 and 20 September. During these three days the burgesses of Egremont were allowed to sell ale without a licence.

By 1800, Egremont was a very different place from the medieval town that had introduced the Crab Fair. It now found itself thriving through the Industrial Revolution, when the waters of the river Ehen powered numerous tanneries and mills. Fewer people now worked in agriculture and for those employed in the mills, leisure time was a rare luxury. By now Egremont Crab Fair had been reduced to a one-day event first held on 19 September and, in 1889, changed again to the 18th. According to a local newspaper at the time this was because the organisers wanted to combine the fair with the local cattle market. This is supported by a number of other sources, which describe the sale of cattle and other animals at the fair as being immensely profitable both to the town and to the neighbouring farmers, who would rent out their land for grazing.

Today, the Crab Fair combines ancient and modern events in a unique way, attracting visitors from all over the world. All the events are traditional, which means that none of them involve any of the mechanical rides that became a big part of country fairs from the late nineteenth century onwards. It is now held on the third Saturday in September, with events starting early in the morning and continuing late into the evening. It is notable for a range of unusual sporting activities, but is perhaps most famous as being the home of the Gurning World Championships.

Gurning competitors have to distort their faces to try and make them as grotesque as possible. They do this in front of a panel of judges with their heads protruding through the middle of a carthorse's collar, or 'braffin'. Gurning contests are known to have been popular in much of rural England and would have been held at fairs up and down the land. There are various suppositions as to the origins of gurning, one of which is that it started when townsfolk would mock the village idiot. A horse's collar would be thrown over him and he would be goaded into pulling funny faces in exchange for ale. Another story relates to a drunken farmer, who, on returning home one night to face the admonishments of his disgruntled wife, thrust a horse collar over her shoulders and exclaimed 'stop gurning woman!' Naturally, her facial expressions became even more enraged and twisted.

Just when the first gurning contest became part of the Egremont Crab Fair is uncertain, but one account claims that the activity here might originate from the effect that eating Baron de Multon's crab apples had on the local people, with their sour, sharp taste. One theory is indeed that the mass gurning competition began after the kindly nobleman enjoyed seeing the contorted faces made by the poor of the parish as they munched into his charitable offerings. Others suggest that it is a much more recent addition, although in 1852 the *Cumberland Paquet* newspaper described it even then as an 'ancient tradition'.

Over the years the event has gone by many names. In 1852 it was described in local newspapers as 'Grin for tobacco', in 1884 it was more colloquially known as 'Grinning for 'bacca'. In the twentieth century it became 'Gurning through a braffin', until finally adopting its current title of 'The Gurning

Gurners at the annual Egremont Crab Fair. (Courtesy of www.egremontcrabfair.com)

World Championships'. The link to tobacco in some of these old names might actually be a clue to its antiquity. The use of tobacco became common in the seventeenth century, when it was either chewed or powdered and inhaled as snuff. So perhaps the introduction of gurning at the Crab Fair dates from these times?

There are now gurning competitions for children, ladies and gentlemen. And although the whole thing might seem a bit daft, some people take it very seriously. For instance, one of the most famous all-time gurners was Peter Jackman, who won the contest four times beginning in 1996 with a face he called his 'Bela Lugosi'. In 2000 he is alleged to have had his teeth deliberately removed to make his features easier to distort. Peter was at the centre of controversy in 1997, when the judges presented first prize to the wrong contestant. Peter Clifford, an actor from Manchester, was initially awarded the title, but afterwards the judges concurred that they had meant Peter Jackman. The situation was resolved a few months later, when the rightful winner was handed the trophy on the television programme *They Think It's All Over*. The last decade and more of Gurning World Championships has been dominated by Tommy Mattinson.

A week or two before the main festivities a Crab Fair Queen is chosen, but the fair and sports themselves usually kick off on the Friday night with a fancy dress wheelbarrow race, a pipe-smoking competition and an evening of live music.

The idea of the pipe smoking is for each competitor to be given a clay pipe filled with tobacco and a box of matches. The person who smokes their tobacco in the quickest time is the winner. The competition used to be held indoors on the Saturday night until smoking was banned in enclosed public spaces. The music evening is one of a number of recent introductions, acknowledging the need to keep the festivities relevant to modern tastes whilst retaining ancient traditional events.

On the Saturday morning one of the most popular events is the greasy pole competition in the Market Place, when competitors scale this slippery shaft to grab a side of mutton. Originally a hat was retrieved from atop the pole, but this was later changed to the lamb. Today there is a permanent pole in the town which was erected specially for the event in 2008, when the traditional wooden pole was replaced by a carbon-fibre structure that has a removable collar designed to prevent people climbing up it at other times. The collar is also designed to hold the traditional side of mutton and to have ribbons tied to it that can be exchanged for small gifts by anyone who is able to claim them.

Further events follow both in the town centre and on Baybarrow Field, which includes the traditional Parade of the Apple Cart. This dates back many hundreds of years, perhaps even to that first fair when Baron de Multon brought a cart of apples to the town. It has always been a popular item in the fair as children scrambled to grab the apples. At one time even cakes were known to have been scattered. Today, eating apples are thrown to the crowd from the back of a van instead of crab apples, so there is no need for distorted faces.

At one time activities such as bull baiting and cock fighting would have been part of the event, but these were banned in 1835. Today, you might observe such events as traditional Cumberland wrestling; children's races; an event known as Riding the Fair; shows for terriers and lurchers, ferrets, poultry and pigeons; and hound dog trails. These are races where hounds have to follow a trail of aniseed scent across the fells – so surely something for everybody.

The origins of Cumberland wrestling are obscure, but it is believed to have been introduced into the area in the tenth century by Viking settlers. Each wrestler locks his hands behind his opponent's back, which is called 'takin' hod'. The object is then to lift your opponent off the ground and throw him down, so that he lands face upwards.

The evening events in the Market Hall start at 6 p.m. with a turn by the town band or a local musician. These include a junior talent contest; the junior gurners; the singing of hunting songs; and horn blowing. The Market Hall is also where the Gurning World Championships get underway at 7 p.m.

Ultimately, the Egremont Crab Fair and Sports is one of the best places left to get an authentic feel of what an old English medieval fair might really have been like, in a contemporary setting.

There are many other unusual sports, games and contests that can be enjoyed around the country and the following are a few examples that you might wish to check out: Dwile Flonking World Championships at Ludham in Norfolk on a Saturday in August; World Coal Carrying Championships at Gawthorpe in Yorkshire on Easter Monday; The Ancient Silver Arrow (The Scorton Arrow Tournament) is held at a different venue in Yorkshire each year, generally in the second half of May; Tetbury Woolsack Races at Tetbury in Gloucestershire on the Whitsun bank holiday Monday; Wenlock Olympian Games at Much Wenlock in Shropshire in early July; Robert Dover's Cotswold Olimpick Games at Chipping Campden in Gloucestershire on the Friday after Spring bank holiday Monday; World Hen Racing Championships at Bonsall in Derbyshire on the first Saturday in August; World Conker Championships at Ashton in Northamptonshire on the second Sunday in October; The World's Biggest Liar Competition at Santon Bridge in Cumbria sometime in November. Not all of these are exactly ancient, and in fact some of them are twentieth-century innovations, but they are all certainly worth a visit.

6

MUMMING

MANY TIMES IN this book you will read the term 'mumming' with regards to the traditional English folk plays that were performed at various times of the year by small groups of plough boys or other farm labourers. These little plays were staged at big houses, village pubs, and even in the intimacy of people's homes. A group of around five or six young farm lads would prowl the village streets just before religious festivals such as Christmas with blackened faces, or face-obscuring masks, and wearing fancy dress. They would knock at doors in the hope of being invited inside to perform their five to ten-minute ritual. This entertainment would normally involve a combat between a hero such as St George, and adversaries with names like Slasher or Hector, which would result in one of the characters being killed and brought back to life by a comical quack doctor. The whole thing would conclude with Beelzebub and Little Devil Doubt going among the audience asking for money, or perhaps more appropriately, food and drink.

These plays would vary slightly around the country but there were basically three main types. First there was the pre-mentioned combat play. Next was the recruiting sergeant's play, most popular on Plough Monday, which was the second Monday in January, or rather the first Monday after Twelfth Night. The story line in this variation, which would also include music and song, involved a farm lad who forswears his sweetheart to join the army. She then decides to marry the village fool, who is one of the other characters in the charade. These plays were most popular in the East Midlands, notably Lincolnshire and Nottinghamshire. Because they were enacted around Plough Monday, the performers were given various names including Plough Stots and

A scene from a Haxby mummers play from the 1920s. The village of Haxby is some 3 miles north of York and the play was performed by village lads on Plough Monday, the second Monday in January. (Courtesy of Peter J. Walls)

Plough Jacks. Some groups were known to take an actual plough with them during their meandering and, similar to the American demand to 'trick or treat' at Halloween, if a person was slow to offer payment, the mummers would threaten to plough up their garden or path.

The third principle variant was the sword dance play, found mainly in the north-east. This drama was largely enacted through dance, during which the fool is executed by the sword dancers. Once again a quack doctor is brought on to revive him, with hilarious results.

In some places mummers adopted regional names, including guisers, rhymers, or pace-eggers, the latter of which are associated mainly with Easter. The actual term 'mummer' derives from an earlier Germanic tradition, where it was coined to describe a 'disguised' or 'masked' person. The mumming groups are generally known as sides. In Cheshire, a variation of this craft was called 'soul caking'. But what exactly was its purpose? Tom Hughes, education officer for Cheshire Museums and erstwhile soul caker himself, explains:

The plays are performed in Cheshire around All Souls' Day, 2nd November. Elsewhere in the country they take place at other religious festivals, such as

Plough Monday in North Yorkshire, and Easter in Lancashire. Some have suggested that the time of year may have a link to which was the most popular festival in that region. However, despite looking into this I have found no evidence to show that All Souls' Day was any more important in Cheshire than any other performance festival. In fact, we might perhaps have expected Whitsun to be chosen, when the mediaeval and Tudor mystery plays were performed in Chester: or Midsummer, when, from 1204 to 1756, all entertainers had to gather at Saint John's church for the Minstrels' Court. The celebration of Halloween in recent years has also led to most soul caking gangs performing their plays around 31st October and several groups, ourselves included, also end up performing in April around Saint George's Day, following requests to provide traditional English entertainments.

All of this helps to explain the mumming calendar, but as for its origins and purpose there is still great controversy, even among its own champions. People spend a lot of time attempting to find some significance to the variations that exist in the plays between villages. But there is likely to be no more significance, Tom Hughes suggests, 'than the antiquarian jotting it down as he remembered it on one particular night.'

Some sources claim that the history of the plays go right back to pre-Christian times and relate to things like the seasons, death and rebirth. However, the documentary evidence does not support this theory, stretching as it does only as far back as the eighteenth century. And yes, 'yawn yawn', some scholars insist that the plays are descended from ancient fertility rituals, as they do for every other custom in the land.

In modern life we have a tendency to look back at old traditions and try to give them some great meaning, while in reality they were often borne out of very practical necessities. Similar to the hodening we spoke of earlier, the performers would go out to big houses at times when farm work was in short supply, simply to be rewarded with food, drink, or money to keep their family fed during some of the leanest periods in the English farming year. When crops failed it was an economic disaster for the landed gentry, while for the 'peasants', for want of a better word, it was potentially a matter of life or death. Under these circumstances mumming could be regarded as little more than begging, while at the same time the labourers were attempting to maintain a sense of dignity and worth. Performing around religious festivals was no doubt intended to appeal to the charitable side of their respective benefactors.

In southern England some of these plays would end with the entrance of a character called 'Little Johnny Jack', who was traditionally played by the youngest or smallest member of the side. This pathetic figure would plead for both food and money on behalf of his wife and children, which were often little more than dolls in a model house, or even a picture.

The name 'soul cakers' derived from the days when the performers would receive beer and 'soul cakes' in return for their dramatic efforts. The soul cakes were small spiced fruit cakes. It is thought that as a person consumed one of these, they would say a prayer for the souls of deceased family and friends. Those who hark back to the pre-Christian ideology, think that cakes would be left out for the souls of the dead to eat at this special time of year.

The group in which Tom Hughes performs is known as 'Jones' Ale Soul Cakers', a name which is borrowed from a now long-defunct folk club. The group can trace its performance history in an unbroken line back to a revival in the 1970s. But, similar to other mumming manifestations, soul caking itself actually dates back to the mid-eighteenth century; the group uses a script that was known to be in existence in 1788. Although being part of an oral tradition, the word 'script' is perhaps a little misleading as every performance will change slightly from the last.

The drama provided by Jones' Ale Soul Cakers is fairly typical of the mumming tradition. It is based on a script that is said to have originated around the

Jones' Ale Soul Cakers perform a traditional play on the city wall in Chester. (Courtesy of Will Riding)

village of Alderley Edge, but also includes a song taken from a souling play from another village near Chester. In bygone centuries the plays were largely performed at big houses or occasionally inns, whereas the modern custom is to take them to traditional English pubs, even though it is becoming increasingly difficult to find venues that fit this description. To announce themselves, the performers stand outside the selected public house and sing a few verses of the song. The 'enterer-in' then steps inside to introduce them and 'clear the way'. Tom Hughes describes what follows:

> Next enters Saint George, who boasts of his many brave deeds and challenges his enemies. In steps Prince Paradise (equivalent to the Turkish knight character common in other folk plays). Paradise challenges George to a sword fight, which provides some of the main focus of the play for the audience. Paradise is wounded but forgiven. Next comes a soldier called Slasher, who challenges and fights George. This time Saint George kills him, then repents and calls for a doctor. In staggers a drunken quack who boasts of his travels and cures, fails comically to cure Slasher, but then with a bottle of 'alec and plain' brings the dead man to life again. The doctor plays his whole scene for laughs and this is really what the audience remembers, as well as being the longest part of the play with the extensive improvisation from all involved. The resurrected Slasher and Saint George fight again, but are silenced by Prince Paradise. After this come other characters who don't really fit into the story of the play. First is Beelzebub, with a monologue of nonsense and dialect oddities, then the groom brings in a skeletal horse and our play ends with more of the song and a request in verse for money or beer. I should mention that our modern collections go to charity.

Although Beelzebub and the skeletal horse do not appear in the main story of the play, in Cheshire at least they have become a key element within the overall mumming experience. Beelzebub certainly appears more frequently in Cheshire than in other parts of England and his mention of 'boggarts', which is a local word for ghosts, also helps to set the scene for the performance to take place around All Souls' Day. The skeletal horse is a traditional hodening horse, which were mentioned in chapter one. Under normal circumstances, farm lads would carry these from door to door at Christmas, similar to carolling. The horse skulls were not easy to prepare and would have been valued by the gangs performing with them. There was tense rivalry between souling gangs who would try to steal each other's skulls because, without them, they would be unable to solicit for beer, cakes or money. Some gangs might also include other characters with no particular relevance to the action, presumably just to provide more roles for any local lads who wanted to be involved. Among the most common of these were Little Devil Doubt, Old Father Christmas, Robin Hood, Old Woman and Old Tosspot. When you consider that the plays were passed from generation to generation by word of mouth, there was a remarkable consistency in character names around the land.

Soul caking was widespread across Cheshire in the late nineteenth century, but as with many other rural customs, it appears to have almost died out by the end of the First World War. There might have been several reasons for this. The most likely being that following the carnage of that conflict, many small farming communities were decimated of their adult male population, a situation that many took a generation to recover from, by which time mechanisation on farms meant that fewer and fewer people were required. Traditional farming life was changing forever, so, inevitably, the customs of rural people would fall victim to these social upheavals. Tom Hughes concludes by stating:

> Antrobus Soul Cakers claim to have the longest unbroken tradition, then nearby Comberbach. Our group – Jones' Ale would be next. Some come and go, but I think the current count is eight gangs of Soul Cakers in Cheshire. Though we play to many new audiences each year who are surprised and then fascinated by the living tradition, there are a number of people who return time and again to see the play enacted once more. With growing interest in English traditions in recent years, I have been asked on several occasions to give talks on the plays. An exhibition on Chester's living traditions was recently held at the Grosvenor Museum in the city and featured our costumes, script and song. Costumes of the short-lived Middlewich Mummers are now on permanent display at the Weaver Hall Museum in Northwich.

As well as the three main strands of play, there are also unique regional variations. A good example of this is the Derby Tup, which is performed around Sheffield and in parts of Derbyshire and Nottinghamshire. 'Tup' is a local word for ram, and this play is a dramatisation of the well-known folk song 'The Derby Ram'. In this short but gruesome performance, one young lad would play the tup (covered in a sack) while carrying a broomstick with a wooden sheep's head attached to it. A butcher would slaughter the animal while another lad held a basin to catch the blood. One popular introduction to the play begins with the words: 'Here comes me an' ahr owd lass, short o' money an' short o' brass: pay for a pint and let us sup, then we'll show yer the Derby Tup.'

The Thameside Mummers parading in Preston Street, Faversham, in Kent, during the 2010 Faversham Hop Festival. (Courtesy of Pam Fray)

Despite the changes to entertainment licencing and the demise of many traditional English public houses which formerly provided the performance venues for mumming groups, it seems that today the practice is very much alive and ready to continue into the future.

Mummers plays should not be confused with mystery plays, which Tom Hughes touched upon earlier, although these even older pieces of amateur dramatics are certainly worthy of a brief mention in their own right.

From the thirteenth century onwards, mystery plays were common all over Europe as a way of celebrating Biblical stories during the feast of Corpus Christi. In England they were most famous around Chester, Coventry, York and Wakefield. The scripts, as in the case of the Chester Cycle, were often written by medieval monks. The plays were originally performed inside churches, but, from the fourteenth century, they were produced by Crafts Guilds and performed in the open streets and market places from the back of pageant carts. They were performed by local people and both the scripts and performances changed each year to remain current and have popular appeal. As with many other forms of religious celebration, the mystery plays were suppressed during the Reformation and the last recorded performance prior to the twentieth-century revivals was in 1575.

7

STRAW BEARS

ONCE, LONG AGO in the town of Whittlesey near Peterborough in Cambridgeshire, it was customary to parade a ploughboy through the streets on the Tuesday after Plough Monday, completely enveloped from head to toe in straw. This 'Straw Bear', as the creation was known, would entertain the townsfolk with frantic and clumsy gestures. The bear's keeper, who led him along by a rope fastened around his chest, would encourage charitable giving by carrying a collecting box and repaying gifts of coinage by making the bear dance. Food and beer would also be gratefully received.

In creating their beast there was a true sense of pride among the ploughing fraternity, who would use only the finest straw. This would be selected during harvesting by the farm workers, who would proclaim, 'that'll do for the bear', as suitable pieces were set aside.

The man or boy chosen to play the bear would have to undergo a remarkable transformation as bands of tightly twisted straw would be wound around his body, arms and legs. These were held in place with twine. He would also have a straw tail attached. But the most impressive part of the costume was the headgear, created by sticks fastened to the shoulders and coming together over the head in a cone-shaped frame that would then be swathed in straw itself. The individual inside the costume would have to be very trusting, for not only was he in danger of catching fire from any unguarded sparks, but he could hardly see anything through his straw mask and could only really go where his keeper led him.

By the beginning of the First World War the custom seems to have fizzled out. However, in 1980 it was revived and is still going strong to this day. The Whittlesea Straw Bear Festival now takes place over three

The Straw Bear is paraded through the streets of Whittlesey during the annual Straw Bear Festival. (Courtesy of James Yardley)

The Straw Bear banner which is carried in the parade at Whittlesey behind the bears. (Courtesy of James Yardley)

days in January (Whittlesea is an older spelling of the town adopted by the festival and, oddly, still displayed at the local railway station, among other uses). As well as the procession of the bear there are displays by morris sides, concerts, storytelling and dances. Strawbearers will go among the crowd with official collecting buckets, selling badges and other memorabilia, and accepting donations in return for programmes. The proceeds, together with money raised from local advertising and dances, goes into the festival's coffers and is used to help pay for the setting-up and running costs associated with this non-profit making event. Any money left over is used within the community.

To understand the origins of the Straw Bear you first have to appreciate the significance of Plough Monday, which we touched upon in the previous chapter. Plough Monday was celebrated on the first Monday after Twelfth Night in areas where the prevailing agriculture was arable, such as Cambridgeshire, Huntingdonshire, Bedfordshire and Northamptonshire. It was once an important date in the rural calendar, being the first day that men resumed work in the fields after Christmas, which suggests that at one time farm labourers in the eastern counties enjoyed a considerable festive break, although this was not their own choice, nor did they have the financial clout to benefit from it.

Plough Sunday, which marked the final flourish of festivities, was celebrated on the first Sunday after Twelfth Night and therefore preceded the return to work of agricultural labourers on Plough Monday. The Plough Sunday custom involved decorating all of the ploughs in the parish with ribbons before pulling them to the church to be blessed by the rector. This practice survives up and down the rural landscape from small villages such as Ston Easton in Somerset, to some of our most illustrious ecclesiastical shrines including Sherborne Abbey in Dorset and Chichester Cathedral. Today, a solitary plough, or even a ploughshare, is blessed in an act intended to benefit all of those involved in the farming world. The following definition of Plough Sunday on the website of Hambledon Valley churches in Buckinghamshire, where an annual service takes place in Turville church, illustrates the concept wonderfully:

> This is a service of prayer, dedication and blessing for all those involved in agriculture and the countryside. It is an opportunity to cherish the land and human labour, and to remind us all of our dependence upon it and upon God.

The earliest known use of the term Plough Monday can be found in a tract by the playwright John Bale (1495-1563) entitled *Yet a Course at the Romyshe Foxe* printed in 1543, which contains the line, 'Than ought my lorde to suffre the same selfe ponnyshment … for not sensinge the plowghes upon Plowgh Mondaye.'

Poet Thomas Tusser (1524-1580) also acknowledges the date in his *Five Hundred Points of Husbandry* written in 1557, in which he notes, 'Plough Munday, next after that Twelf-tide is past, Bids out with the plough; the worst husband is last.' Plough Monday is subsequently mentioned in several other historical texts, as the time of year when ploughing and other rustic toils recommenced. However, it seems that at some juncture it degenerated from being a day of work, to a day when gangs of men attempted to procure funds by other means, when it is hard to believe that any work was done.

In his booklet *Whittlesey Straw Bear*, published in 1989, George Frampton describes Plough Monday as 'an occasion to procure money or largesse in a token pageant'. He describes how plough gangs in Eastern England would proceed between large houses, shops and the like, pulling a plough adorned with ribbons, which was referred to as the Fool Plough. Anyone who was slow in putting their hands in their pockets would be threatened with reprisals, such as having their lawn or dunghill ploughed up. Most people therefore responded positively to the request of 'just one for the poor ploughboy'.

At a time when there were no paid holidays, this act of begging coincided with a period of both agricultural inactivity, when labourers were unable to earn money, and festive spending, when all of their financial reserves had dwindled. As we have already established through mumming, there were many forms of cadging, the crudest known as 'mumping' or 'lomping'. This was when groups of stick-wielding men in disguises would simply prowl the streets at night chanting 'Mump! Mump! Mump!' or alternatively, 'Lomp! Lomp! Lomp! If you don't give me something, I'll give you a good crump.'

In all such activities disguise was integral, as men did not want to be recognised by potential employers, so they blacked their faces, dressed as women, or, later, Red Indians. Many processions with ploughs would include someone dressed as an old woman called 'Bessy' who carried a collecting box. Another character was 'The Fool', said to have been completely dressed in animal skins and having a long tail. Was this perhaps an inspiration for straw bears? At Godmanchester, men were known to stuff straw down the back of their jackets or shirts, to give themselves a grotesque hump-backed appearance. Perhaps another clue?

For hundreds of years the fortunes of agricultural workers in this country changed considerably, often for the worst, and Plough Monday was probably never regarded as a day of celebration but rather a chance to secure funds to feed the families of farm workers at a time when employment was scarce. However, with the passing of time the occasion became more disreputable, until gangs of genuine ploughmen found themselves competing for charitable donations against other local entrepreneurs, who saw this as a chance of making easy money. These often menacing rivals, who the press of the day accused of being 'men who never plough', were often drunk and disorderly and contributed to giving the custom a bad name, which resulted in turning communities against the practice.

Plough Monday was celebrated in various ways in different places, although the incidence of straw bears seems to have been unique to the Fenland towns of Ramsey and Whittlesey. At Ramsey, records only establish the existence of straw bears around the 1870s and '80s, suggesting that their animal was merely an imitation of the older Whittlesey craft. In the latter town, the bear did not appear on Plough Monday itself, but on the following day, which became known as Straw Bear Day.

The first known written account of the Whittlesey Bear appeared in the *Peterborough Advertiser* in 1859, the reporter suggesting that these were the same parties that went out on Plough Monday, although this time enveloped in straw, who 'levied blackmail with intolerable impartiality on the inhabitants'. Over the next few decades the celebration seems to have been somewhat sporadic, which might have been to do with the availability of work. What is certain is that there were often several bears, not just one. An article in the *Cambridge Times and March Gazette* in 1887 notes:

> Tuesday was Straw Bear Day and though the morning being wet, there were not so many bears on exhibition as usual. One very fine and mischievous animal known by the name of 'William-Burgess' was exhibited by its owner Mr Billing, and responded freely to its masters' demand for another dance and a growl by way of recognition for anything bestowed upon it. But the one that took the blue ribbon was Mr Anker's well-known 'Bobbedford' which showed off in his usual form, and received the praise of all who saw him.

These straw bears, together with their handlers, would prowl the streets and make house calls in the hope of procuring a penny or two. The local children were known to chase them and try to take prized-possession of their tails. Their last confirmed sighting possibly comes from the *Whittlesey Guardian and County Press* in 1913, and it would appear that even then the custom was 'fast dying out'. Perhaps the date in question is crucial to the bear's fate, as the First World War not only robbed the country of so many young men from rural areas, but likewise their traditions. Having said that, eyewitness accounts from the time also suggest that the local police authorities tried to ban the practice on several occasions because it always seemed to result in unruliness.

Although there are unofficial accounts of straw bears appearing intermittently as late as the 1930s, for several reasons they were eventually consigned to the pages of history.

Peter Williams, the director of the festival between 2008 and 2011, makes the interesting point that, probably similar to the organisers of many of the other customs we have seen, red tape sometimes makes you forget how the whole thing began:

> When you are involved in organising a festival that takes the best part of a year, as director one tends to concentrate on the mechanics of getting the show on the road with a thousand and one jobs to be done and also having to fight bureaucracy, comply with health and safety, apply for licences etc., need I go on. We all perhaps miss the simple origins a little and why we are doing it. I often wonder how long it took our forefathers to organise the Straw Bear Day back in the late 1800s. No more than a couple of days I bet.

The inaugural Straw Bear Festival in 1980 was inspired by a number of things, one of which was the opening of a new public house in Whittlesey in 1975. The *Peterborough Evening Telegraph* ran a competition to find a suitable name for the establishment and The Straw Bear was chosen. Two years later, in 1977, a brace of bears took part in a parade through the town to mark the Queen's Silver Jubilee. Another inspiration came from the revival of old English folk music occurring at that time, from which emerged an album by Ashley Hutchings entitled *Rattlebone and Ploughjack*, released by Island Records in 1976, which included a spoken description of the original custom. Collectively all of this prompted Brian Kell, who at the time was a member of the Peterborough Morris Men and the Whittlesea Society, to suggest reviving the Straw Bear.

Having met with the approval of the Whittlesea Society and the wider community, the first revival took place on 12 January 1980, the Saturday before Plough Monday. Brian Kell played the part of the bear, wearing a suit of straw attached to a substrate made from a boiler suit. The head was detachable, so it could be lifted off at intervals to enable a welcome drink.

The procession went from Whittlesey Museum at 10.30 a.m. to the Market Place, where there were displays of morris and other traditional dance. The bear himself had no musical accompaniment during this first outing. Also making an appearance was Sylvester, the Peterborough Hobby Horse, a creature topped by an enormous reindeer's head. During the remainder of the festival the bear danced en route and at several hostelries, which is no doubt where the detachable head was most appreciated. A lunch was also enjoyed at St Mary's Parish Rooms, put on by the Whittlesea Society, as well as a rousing evening of traditional song and dance at the same venue. Events continued into Plough Sunday and concluded at the Nag's Head at Eastrea. It proved to be a successful and popular reincarnation, in some part due to the coverage it received through local newspapers, television and radio.

The current festival takes place over the second weekend in January, starting on the Friday evening with a concert at the Ivy Leaf Club. On the Saturday the bear processes around the streets with its keeper and musicians, and dances to a tune which was featured on Ashley Hutchings' album. They are followed by numerous dance sides, mainly visitors, including morris men and women, molly, rapper, longsword and clog dancers, who perform at various points along the route. Today there is also a smaller bear, in which a child is ensconced. Sessions of traditional music take place in many of the town's public houses during the day and evening, and a barn dance or ceilidh, followed by a Cajun dance, round off the Saturday night. On Sunday there is further music and dance before the bear costume is ceremonially set alight.

Because of this burning of the bear, some written sources now suggest that the festival is descended from some pagan ritual, where a man dressed in straw was sacrificed to promote the harvest. But this is fanciful and highly unlikely. As we have seen, records only date the event to the mid-Victorian period and these seem to suggest that it was merely practised as a form of cadging, to help farm workers supplement their meagre earnings at a time of need. Apart from that, Brian and Christine Kell, who have been involved with the revival from its onset, confirm, 'it is simply to get rid of the straw and end the festival. We used to just burn it at the bottom of someone's garden, which was just as sociable with a half dozen of us.'

At Carshalton in Surrey, a not dissimilar creation is their Straw Jack, who is paraded and dances in September as a celebration of harvest. Here a straw man is made and later burnt at the end of his travels, during which he is accompanied by musicians, drummers, sweepers, and characters such as the Reaper Man, Corn Dollies, the Rat Catcher, the Squire, the Cider Man, the Scarecrow, and the Milk Maid. Of course by the time Jack is burnt, the person inside has already been stripped of the straw suit.

8

WASSAILING

THE TRADITION OF Wassailing can be quite confusing, as it relates to a number of separate customs with some common ground. It is also associated with two different tipples, ale and cider. In its most basic semblance, wassail is an ale-based beverage seasoned with spices. This warming punch would be mixed in a large bowl at Christmas or New Year and passed around family and friends, with the greeting 'wassail' as a blessing of good health. This might be done in the home, an alehouse, or some other venue where like-minded souls gathered at festive times. The bowl itself was often referred to as a 'loving cup'. So the wassail was the name of both the drink and the greeting.

The origin of the term was either Norse or Anglo-Saxon, both of which had variations of the same custom and, of course, both of these ancient societies settled in and influenced parts of Britain. The Vikings would welcome guests by passing a horn of ale among them and using the phrase '*ves heill*', meaning 'be healthy'. The Saxons on the other hand regaled their guests with a goblet of mead and the greeting '*wæs hal*', again wishing good health.

At the beginning of each year the Saxon manorial lords were known to summon their serfs together and bless them with a shout of '*wæs hal*', to which the gathered throng were expected to offer the response '*drinc hal*', meaning 'drink and be healthy'. In time this led to '*wæs hal*' being used as an everyday greeting in Anglo-Saxon society. As the centuries passed the phrase was merged into the single old English word 'wassail' and was generally used as a way of toasting someone's well-being at times of special celebration.

The use of a wassail bowl at Christmas and New Year can certainly be traced back to the 1400s. The custom became very popular among the good and great of the land and in wealthier abodes the wassail bowl could be quite elaborate, sometimes made of pewter or even silver, although more traditionally of clay or wood. It reached its height of popularity during the seventeenth century, when the aristocracy and landed gentry really took it to their hearts. Large houses and country estates demanded magnificent bowls to grace their Christmas tables, which stood elevated on a stemmed foot looking like a huge chalice.

These bowls were often turned from a single piece of timber, *Lignum Vitea*, which had only recently been discovered and introduced into Britain from South America. Others were made from white maple. In the Christmas carol 'Wassail, wassail, all over the town', the singers tell that their 'bowl it is made of the white maple tree'. This is a completely tasteless wood, often used even today to fashion some kitchen utensils, and it was likely that many simple peasant wassail bowls were turned from it.

But as well as prominent families, other important bodies and institutions would possess their own grand vessels, sometimes embellished with finely carved ornamentation. The Worshipful Company of Grocers, for instance, made a very elaborate one in the seventeenth century decorated with silver. There were also puzzle wassail bowls containing several spouts. As you attempted to drink from one spout, you would find yourself being drenched by liquid gushing out of another, much to the ribaldry of your companions.

The contents of the bowl varied around the land depending on local ingredients, but a popular brew was known as 'Lamb's Wool'. This was a concoction of hot ale, roasted crab apples, spices, eggs, sugar and cream. Little pieces of toast floated on the surface and it was these that gave the drink its unusual name.

With the further passing of time the tradition sprouted a secondary shoot, in which groups of people proceeded to large houses around Christmas time bearing a wassail bowl of hot spiced ale and singing wassailing songs. In similar fashion to hodening or mumming they hoped to receive money, drink or festive fare. Home dwellers would offer the wassailers mince pies, figgy pudding or the like, in the belief that this act of kindness would afford themselves good luck in the coming year.

This form of wassailing became increasingly popular, with groups going from door to door in towns and villages performing what was in effect an early type of carol singing. A few songs descended from this tradition have become catalogued as traditional Christmas carols, such as 'Here we come a-wassailing, among the leaves so green'. These wassailing carols were unusual because they did not praise the nativity but were nevertheless Christian in their theme and lyrics, constantly giving thanks to God.

Again similar to mumming, the wassailers did not want to give the impression that they were begging, so the singing of songs and presentation of the wassail bowl was in exchange for charity. This point is stressed in the same carol which contains the words: 'We are not beggars that beg from door to door, but we are friendly neighbours whom you have seen before.' Should they be rewarded, they would then serenade their benefactors with the following blessing of goodwill:

> Love and joy come to you
> And to you your wassail too,
> And God bless you and send you
> A Happy New Year.

In these ancient refrains we can very clearly see the evolution of Christmas carols such as 'We wish you a Merry Christmas', which largely date from the sixteenth century. The first carols to appear in English were published in a work of 1426 by John Awdlay, a Shropshire chaplain who listed twenty-five examples in his *Caroles of Cristemas*, collected from wassailing groups. Carols were not sung in churches until much later.

Across the country children and adults still go out carol singing before Christmas, usually to raise money for local charities and in most cases blissfully unaware that their actions, now taken for granted as part of our annual festive pomp, are a descendent form of the wassailing carried out by their ancestors.

Although door-to-door wassailing is often depicted as a charming reminder of a vanished way of life, in England it was not always regarded with the innocence that nostalgia might suggest. The practice became associated with drunken young men, who, in gangs and no doubt intoxicated by their own wassail, would enter people's homes with little or no invitation, demanding payment for a few tuneless bars. If the victim refused, then in trick-or-treat style they would be cursed. And if things turned really nasty, they might even find their homes revisited at a later hour and vandalised.

Perhaps this more sinister trait is hinted at in the aforementioned carol, when the performers demand 'oh, bring us a figgy pudding and a cup of good cheer,' stating, 'we won't go until we get some, so bring some out here!' This may not seem very threatening when sung by a choir of five year olds in woolly hats, earmuffs and scarves, but when confronted by a rowdy gang of eighteenth-century drunken ploughboys with bulging biceps, it might have been taken a little more seriously.

Another variation of the custom, still prevalent today and the one that most people now know, was Apple Tree Wassailing, which involved going to an orchard and drinking the health of the cider apple trees. As can be imagined this was most popular in the cider-producing counties of the SouthWest and West of England, including Somerset, Devon, Dorset, Gloucestershire and Herefordshire. In these counties you will still observe the ritual performed in the orchards of cider makers, among other places.

In earlier times, when the countryside was blessed with more farms and many more people worked in agriculture, there were obviously a greater number of orchards, in fact most farms would have had their own. Some farm workers even received cider as a part of their wages. This made Apple Tree Wassailing quite an important event in the rural calendar, observed by most of the village in the same way that harvesting came to be a communal event.

Although wassailing today is associated almost solely with cider apples, it is probable that if you went back hundreds of years and to different parts of the country, other crops and fruits, perhaps even livestock, would have been the subject of similar tributes. People would no doubt have gathered to wish the health of plums, pears, or anything else that helped to provide sustenance for the community. The following ancient refrain bears testimony to this:

> Wassaile the trees that they may beare
> You many a plum and many a pear
> For more or less fruits they will bring
> As you do give them wassailing.

The practice varies slightly from place to place but during a typical ceremony a wassailing bowl would be carried from orchard to orchard by a procession of people led by the Wassail King and Queen, from which some of the contents would be sprinkled over the apple trees to promote a bountiful crop. In former times the drink might have been spiced ale, but today it is more likely to be some of the orchard's own mulled scrumpy.

Within the orchard a particular tree would then be selected, perhaps the biggest one with a past history of bumper yields, or simply the oldest and most revered. The Wassail Queen would be lifted up into the boughs of the tree and would place pieces of cider-soaked toast into the forks of its branches. Cider would also be poured over its roots to show it some of the fruits produced the previous year. The assembled company would then recite an incantation to encourage a good apple harvest, such as the following from the South Hams of Devon, recorded in 1871:

Here's to thee, old apple tree,
Whence thou mayst bud
And whence thou mayst blow!
And whence thou mayst bear apples enow!
Hats full! Caps full!
Bushel – bushel – sacks full,
And my pockets full too! Huzza!

The villagers would go armed with pots, pans, drums, or anything else capable of creating a tremendous din, aimed at raising the sleeping spirits of the orchard and chasing off demons. In some places the men would howl like banshees, at the top of their voices. Then, as firearms became available to farmers, a volley of musket shot would also be fired through the branches, while today the common practice is to ward off evil with the use of shotguns. In practical terms, evil spirits were manifested in maggots and worms, while the robin was seen as the personification of the good spirit.

Apple Tree Wassailing was first recorded at Fordwich in Kent in 1585, when it seems that groups of young men went between orchards performing for rewards, but of course it would have been much older than that. By the 1670s John Aubrey, the English writer and antiquary, described how in the West Country on Twelfth Night, 'men go with their wassel-bowl into the orchard and go about the trees to bless them, and put a piece of toast upon the roots.'

Traditionally, the ceremony was held on the eve of Twelfth Night, or Old Christmas Eve which, although the subject is of much debate, is correctly the evening of 5 January. However, most wassailing will take place on 'Old Twelvey Night' – 17 January – as that would have been the correct date before the introduction of the Gregorian Calendar in 1752.

There are still many places where wassailing is observed. The longest running event in Somerset has been held annually on 17 January for the last 150 years, at the Butchers Arms in Carhampton. The land behind the pub was once a thriving orchard which was sold off in the 1970s for housing development. A few apple trees remain on the pub's property and the locals continue to honour them just as their ancestors have done for many decades.

But there are many more examples, such as the Apple Howling on Old Mill Farm, Bolney in Sussex, which takes place on the first Saturday in January. This includes a torchlight procession and 'general hullabaloo'. The spectators are encouraged to bring their own dustbin lids, rattles and whistles to create as much noise as possible. The largest event in Sussex is the Firle Wassail on the second Saturday of the year at Middle Farm near Lewes.

During apple tree wassailing the roots of the chosen tree are anointed with cider to put some goodness back into the soil. (© Glyn Baker)

Cider-soaked toast is placed in the branches of an apple tree to attract evil spirits. The hope is for robins to eat the toast and carry the evil away. (© Glyn Baker)

Wassailers at Maplehurst in West Sussex beat an apple tree with sticks in John Bacheldor's apple orchard, to drive out any evil spirits that may spoil the crop. (© Glyn Baker)

After the wassail at Maplehurst, the Broadwood Morris Dancers play in the White Horse, where the evening's festivities also began. (© Glyn Baker)

Another large ceremony is the Whimple Wassail in Devon, held on 17 January. This well-supported event passes between a number of orchards, ending at the cricket club. Again participants are encouraged to enter into the spirit of the evening by wearing traditional dress and bringing instruments that will make sufficient noise to waken the trees and ward off evil.

Other events take place at farms and orchards across the country, as well as National Trust and other similar establishments. Many are big events with bonfires, barn dances, musical entertainment and suppers. You will usually find them well advertised in your local press.

Another custom related to wassailing was known as 'burning the ashen faggot', or sometimes the 'Ashton faggot'. This was a West Country oddity which was widespread in both Somerset and Devon, particularly on and around Dartmoor. It varied around the region but it was in Somerset where it was most strongly associated with the former custom and, once again, its origins filtered down from Anglo-Saxon and Norse mythology.

A faggot is basically an old English term for a bundle of sticks gathered to burn on the fire; so an ashen faggot was comprised of twigs cut from an ash tree.

In ancient lore the ash was believed to have magical qualities. The Vikings considered it to be the tree of life and during their feast of Joul, they would burn huge bonfires of ash in celebration of their god Thor. They revered one immense tree called 'Yggdrasil', which was central to Norse cosmology. This 'World Ash Tree' was at the heart of their existence, its branches rose up to the heavens while its roots descended deep into the underworld. Many mythological creatures lived within its reaches, including 'Wyrm' the dragon. In old Norse the word '*Yggdrasil*' translates as 'Odin's horse', Odin being the principle god of north Germanic tradition.

The West Country writer Revd Sabine Baring-Gold (1834-1924), who came from the Okehampton area, catalogued many local customs in his works and in his novel *Glámr* he described how the ceremony might have been practised in large houses in Saxon England on Christmas Eve:

> There the great ashen faggot is rolled along the hall with torch and taper; the mummers dance with their merry jingling bells; the boar's head with gilded tusks, bedecked with holly and rosemary, is brought in by the steward to a flourish of trumpets.

In later times the tradition was certainly not as grand as this and was performed in alehouses, farmhouses, or other places large enough to support an inglenook or similar fireplace.

In the more recent tradition, the faggot would be bound with nine lengths of green ash bands known as 'beams', all cut from the same tree. The fire would be lit on Christmas Eve using the salvaged remains of the previous year's faggot for kindling. Once the fire was going the new faggot would be placed on top, while those gathered watched it burn with deep interest. Some sources maintain that the salvaged remains were actually placed in the centre of the new faggot, illustrating how customs varied from place to place.

Burning the ashen faggot was supposed to bring the household good fortune in the coming year, but, just as importantly, bad luck would befall any households that did not observe the custom.

Unmarried women among the watchers would choose one of the bindings and it is believed that the maiden who selected the first band to burst would be the next to get married. As each binding broke, a toast would be made and cider passed around, often laced with brandy.

Some records of the custom state that once the fire was well alight and the wood beginning to crack, the youngest child of the household would be placed on top of the faggot. How long the child remained there was seen by the elders to be an indication of their future courage.

Once all the bindings had burst the faggot would fall apart and anybody who intended to host a similar event next year would quickly retrieve one of the half-burned ash sticks in order to light their own fire the following Christmas. The rest of the evening would then be spent in revelry, eating, drinking, dancing, singing and telling stories.

On Dartmoor this was normally done on Christmas Eve, while in parts of Somerset it would fall in line with wassailing, taking place on 5 January, or more commonly 17 January. Where the custom is known as the Ashton faggot the term may derive from Ashburton on Dartmoor, where it was said to be particularly well supported. In 1878, no fewer than thirty-two farms and cottages here were recorded as having burned a faggot.

There are many thoughts as to why a Christian society adopted what was so evidently a pagan ritual. One of these comes from Romany lore, which claims that Jesus was born in a field, not a stable, and was kept warm by an ash fire lit by the Virgin Mary.

Places that still observe the custom publicly include the Harbour Inn at Axmouth in Devon, and the Shave Cross Inn near Bridport in Dorset. In Somerset, the Curry Rivel Wassailers keep the ceremony alive in the King William pub and have done so for at least 150 years. In former times the faggot would be lit on Old Christmas Eve and kept alight during the twelve days of Christmas. As it died down, the wassailers would go to the orchards to toast the apple trees. Today the pub is the final stop on the annual wassail. The group returns here after several house calls have been made, during which residents are treated to the wassail song.

Pubs all over the region have reintroduced the custom in recent times, combining the burning of the ashen faggot with music, dancing, food and drink, all of which are designed to lure punters in to the premises on a cold winter's night.

Of course there are similarities in all of this to another Christmas custom, that of burning the Yule Log; not to be confused with the chocolate-covered cake bought at supermarkets during the festive season.

This particular custom was much more widespread in northern Europe, although it did have followings all over England, where it was known by many different names. In the West Country it was called 'Yule Block'; in Cornwall 'Stock of the Mock'; in Lincolnshire 'Gule Block'; and in the north-east 'Yule Clog'.

In its original form this involved the felling of an entire tree, which was then brought in to the farmhouse with great aplomb. The origin was possibly Anglo-Saxon Germanic and undoubtedly pagan, although here in Britain it was probably always a Christian dedication. Choosing such a large log at this time of year was practical as well as symbolic, as it provided the farmhouse with maximum heat and burning endurance.

How an entire tree was placed on a hearth is unclear, but some sources note that the largest end of the tree would be placed in the fire while the rest of it stuck out into the room. Presumably as it burned and shortened, the tree would have been pushed along the floor. In older halls and large farmhouses an open hearth might have dominated the centre of the room, which would have made the practice more feasible.

The first recorded mention of the custom in Britain was from the writings of Robert Herrick (1591-1674), who was an English poet and at one time the vicar of Dean Prior in Devon. He called it a 'Christmas log' and described how this item was brought into the farmhouse by a group of men who were then rewarded with ale from the farmer's wife.

Very similar to the ashen faggot, Herrick explained that the fire was started by burning a remnant from the previous year's log and that the idea behind the custom was to bring prosperity to the house and protect it from evil. The custom died out in rural Britain in the late nineteenth and early twentieth centuries and has never, to my knowledge, been seriously revived.

9

FLITCH TRIALS

FLITCH TRIALS RANK among our most ancient ceremonies and are responsible for giving our language the expression 'bringing home the bacon'. A flitch itself is half a pig, smoked and preserved, and in mediaeval times it would have been considered a colossal prize, providing enough meat to feed a family through much of the winter.

The most famous of all flitch trials takes place once every leap year at the town of Great Dunmow in Essex. It was traditionally held on Whit Monday, but the modern event is now held on a Saturday in July. In order to win the bacon, married couples have to prove their devotion to one another before a judge, who is a local dignitary, and a jury consisting of six bachelors and six spinsters from the parish of Great Dunmow. To qualify as claimants, the couples must have been married for at least one year and a day. And here's the tricky part – they have to prove that during that time they have lived in complete harmony and never wished themselves unwed.

Half a pig might not seem a particularly romantic reward for such devotion but apparently the flitch was regarded by both the Romans and the Saxons as a symbol of fertility. So it is possible that some semblance of this custom might have been performed in England as long as 2,000 years ago.

On the day of the trials, the court holds session in a large marquee erected in the town. Five couples would have been pre-selected to face cross-examination and their trials take place throughout the day: one trial in the morning, two in the afternoon, and two in the evening. It is not a competition and each of the couples can succeed in claiming a flitch, should the jury feel disposed to believing their testimony.

The idea behind employing bachelors and spinsters in the jury is that they have some kind of impartiality, making them the best judge of whether or not two people seem contented. In order to prove their case, the couples have a leading counsel and an assistant to speak up for them, while the donors of the bacon have the same, whose job is to try and trip the couples up.

Early each leap year, couples – now from all around the world – apply to take part in the trials. Anyone is welcome to apply assuming they meet all the criteria, and as long as their wedding was a legally recognised religious or civil ceremony. After sifting through all the applications with careful consideration, a shortlist is drawn up of couples who are then invited to attend an interview with their prospective judge, his chaplain, and the Mayor of Great Dunmow. From these interviews, the final pairings are selected.

Friar Bacon, a leading authority on the trials and author of the 2008 booklet, *The Dunmow Flitch*, wrote:

> Although the couples know when they are being selected, secrecy is maintained as to their identity until the day of the Trial. The reason for this is that in the past there was a couple who were selected and there was publicity in their home town leading up to the Trials. Unfortunately their son died a few days before the Trials so obviously they felt that they could not take part and not only had their grief to cope with but also the enquiries as to how they got on.

Friar Bacon, I should point out, if you have not already guessed, is a pen name. In fact that of two people, both heavily involved with the present tradition: Peter Street the chairman of the Dunmow and District Historical and Literary Society, and Michael Chapman, the president of the said society. The latter is also a solicitor and deputy lieutenant of the county of Essex. He is also the judge that couples currently face at their Flitch Trial, having apprenticed as a junior counsel since the 1980s. We shall be hearing from them – or him – again later.

On the day of the trials, much of Great Dunmow comes to a standstill as a procession makes its way through the town, starting outside the Saracen's Head Hotel, a sixteenth-century coaching inn, and finishing at the marquee in which the court is to be held. The parade adheres to a strict order, with the Town Crier at its head, ringing his bell and making announcements as he proceeds. Next in line is the flitch, which is hanging from a wooden frame decorated with garlands of flowers, including one wrapped around the bacon itself. This is carried on the shoulders of four stout fellows each attired in traditional Essex smocks.

Following the flitch are the court usher, the clerk of the court, and the counsels for and against the claimants. Next up are the claimants themselves, seated in a great wooden chair, again carried on the shoulders of eight men in traditional attire. Finally come the jury, the judge's chaplain, and the judge.

When everybody has at last arrived in court, the jury is sworn in, just as they would be in a Crown court, and the opening couple are called forward to stand in the dock. They first have to present their case through their counsel, who will make the history of their relationship known, explaining how they met and courted, how and where they were married, and describing the concord of their subsequent union. They are then cross-examined to establish their complete compatibility with one another. The counsel for the bacon employs all sorts of tricks to find fault with their claim, probing for inconsistencies or disagreements between them. When all avenues have been explored, the counsels for and against, and the judge himself, give their final summing up to the jury, which then retires to consider their verdict.

Once the jury has made their decision based on the facts presented to them, they return to the court and deliver their verdict. By no means are all couples successful. Those who are unsuccessful in their claim have to walk through the town to the Market Place, following the empty flitch chair. Here they are presented with a gammon: in itself not a bad prize. Successful claimants on the other hand are carried through the town in the flitch chair. Having arrived at the Market Place they have to kneel on pointed stones and take the ancient oath, whereupon they are finally presented with their flitch.

FLITCH OATH

> You doe swear by custom of confession
> That you ne're made Nuptiall Transgression,
> Nor since you were married man and wife,
> By household brawles or contentious strife
> Or otherwise in bed or at boarde,
> Offended each other in Deed or in Word
> Or in a twelve moneths time and a day
> Repented not in thought in any way
> Or since the Church Clerke said Amen
> Wish't yourselves unmarried agen,
> But continue true and in desire,
> As when you joyn'd hands in Holy Quire.

Flitch winners Chris and Catherine Metson being chaired through Great Dunmow in 1984. Catherine comes from a family of flitch winners, the first being her grandparents in 1949. Her parents-in-law were winners in 1954. (Courtesy of Catherine Metson)

In 1949, Catherine Metson's grandparents Laura and Bill Lews went through the whole ceremony themselves. (Courtesy of Catherine Metson)

Claire Raynor was Chris and Catherine Metson's counsellor for the claimants. Catherine explains: 'We met her beforehand to talk about our marriage and life together. How we met, how we coped with differences etc. Who had the last say in our relationship and so on. It was her job to prove we were a happy couple who never wished ourselves unwed.' (Courtesy of Catherine Metson)

THE SENTENCE

Since to these Conditions without any fear,
Of your own accords you doe freely Swear,
A Whole Flitche of Bacon you doe receive,
And beare it away with Love and good Leave,
For this is the Custome of Dunmow well known,
Tho' the Pleasure be Ours, the Bacon's your own.

These particular flitch trials have not always taken place at Great Dunmow. In fact, they were inaugurated at the nearby village of Little Dunmow and the present ceremony can be traced back to the time of the Norman Conquest. Following Duke William's successful invasion of Britain, he rewarded his trusted knights with the gift of land. The manor of Little Dunmow was given to a man called Ralph Baynard. Ralph had a sister called Lady Juga (or Jauga), who founded a church in the manor which was consecrated in 1104 by Bishop Morris of London, and which in 1106 was upgraded to an Augustinian priory. Tradition states that both Prioress Juga and Bishop Morris were so worried about the reluctance of local people to enter into the institution of Christian marriage, that it was they who had the idea of rewarding couples with a flitch, if they could prove they had been happily married for a year and a day.

But why a flitch? As previously stated, the flitch was regarded as a fertility symbol to the pre-Norman inhabitants of the realm. So it is quite probable that they continued, or at least revived a more ancient ceremonial. Of course today very little remains of the priory at Little Dunmow, which was destroyed at the time of Henry VIII's Reformation, when much of its masonry was taken away by local lords and farmers to build their own properties. All that remains of it now is the small Lady Chapel that is today used as the parish church of Little Dunmow, St Mary the Virgin's.

So the Dunmow Flitch has a long and colourful history, with many references made to it in English literature. By the mid-1300s it had certainly established some fame. As far away as Shropshire, the poet William Langland (1332-1386) mentions it in his *The Vision of Piers Ploughman*, in which he writes: 'Though they ride in Dunmow, unless the devil help them. To fetch the Flitch, they will fail to get it; Unless both be forsworn, the bacon is another's …'

It is interesting to note that Langland gives the reader no explanation of what the Dunmow Flitch was, leading Friar Bacon to deduce, 'it must have been part of every reader's general knowledge.' The same principle must therefore apply when Geoffrey Chaucer (1343-1400) also mentions the trials in 'The Wife of Bath's Tale', one of his famous *Canterbury Tales*. This particular pilgrim, travelling to the shrine of St Thomas Beckett, was noted for having had five husbands, all of which she famously kept under her thumb. She says: 'I set them so to work I'm bound to say; Many a night they sang, "Alack the day!" Never for them the Flitch of Bacon though, That some have won in Essex at Dunmow!'

The first recorded winner of the flitch of bacon is one Richard Wright, a yeoman of Badbourge in Norfolk. His name can be found on a document contained in the British Museum, the date given as 27 April 1445. What the document does not record is the name of his wife, and the same thing applies in several subsequent entries. The reason for this we do not know, but it is quite likely that women, other than the Prioress herself and other ecclesiastical servants, were not allowed within the priory walls, so the evidence to win these early flitches was possibly given from a male perspective only.

After the dissolution of the monasteries (1536-1540) the custom seems to have lapsed and was not revived again properly until 7 June 1701, when, under the patronage of Sir Thomas May, two couples were awarded the bacon: John and Anne Reynolds of Hatfield Broad Oak, Essex, and William and Jane Parsley of Much Easton, Essex. For the first time a jury decided on the awards, and at last we are regularly given the name of the wife. By profession, Reynolds was a steward to Sir Charles Barrington, while Parsley was a butcher – quite apt really.

Over the coming years, controversy occasionally courted the ceremony, which came to a head on 20 June 1751 with the infamous trial of Thomas and Anne Shakeshaft, at the time when Mary Hallett, the widow of James Hallet, was lady of the manor. Shakeshaft was a weaver from Wethersfield in Essex, and after being awarded the bacon, he and his wife cut it up into slices and sold it to the many sightseers who had flocked to the trial, at handsome prices: rather defeating the object. It seems that after this fiasco, the lords of the manor lost interest in the affair and for a while it was neglected.

Although there were one or two attempts to reinstate the flitch trials, they remained in the wilderness until the 1850s. One successful attempt was made in 1851, when Mr and Mrs Hurrell of Felsted in Essex made a claim to the lord of the manor of Dunmow Priory, who refused to grant it. When the refusal became known to the people of Dunmow, they decided to take matters into their own hands and sent the Hurrells a letter, to the effect that if they attended a public fête at Great Dunmow, on 16 July, they would receive a gammon of bacon as a prize if they took the customary and ancient oath. In a booklet published in 1855, Charles Pavey wrote of the event:

> This notification being given to Mr and Mrs Hurrell, harmony was at once restored to the good folks of Dunmow, some of whom were afraid the Custom would be extinguished. A capital Brass Band was engaged, who mustered opposite the Town Hall, and when the happy Couple arrived at the Market Cross, at (Great) Dunmow, they were received with joyful strains, as well as the acclamations of a large assemblage. Plenty of strong ale, and good fat beef, had been provided for their entertainment, at the Three Tuns Inn, at Dunmow, on their return. At three o'clock, the neighbours and friends crowded to the Market Cross, at Dunmow, to accompany Mr and Mrs Hurrell to the park, proving that the joyous Couple possessed the hearty sympathy of all who knew them.

The final destination of this procession was the agricultural fête held in Easton Park, where roughly 3,000 people, including members of the local aristocracy, witnessed and congratulated them as they took the oath. Afterwards, having received the bacon, the couple drove out of the park gates in their chaise, as the band played 'Oh dear, what can the matter be'. As a result of this quiet public revolution, the Dunmow Flitch Trials were forever transplanted from Little to Great Dunmow.

In 1854, the author Harrison Ainsworth published a novel entitled *The Custom of Dunmow*. The book features the publican at the Flitch of Bacon

1 The Hobby Horse appears every Spring Bank Holiday weekend in the North Devon village of Combe Martin. (Courtesy of Earl of Rone Council)

2 The 'fine lady' on her white horse is now an established fixture in the annual Banbury Hobby Horse Festival. (Courtesy of Sandy Glover)

3 The Earl of Rone is paraded through the village of Combe Martin in Devon on Spring Bank Holiday Monday, sitting back to front on a garlanded donkey after his capture by Grenadiers. (Courtesy of Earl of Rone Council)

4 Running the annual Pancake Race at Olney in Buckinghamshire, where this national pastime is said to have begun. (Courtesy of Michael Brace)

5 This photograph gives a good impression of the huge gathering that takes part in Ashbourne's annual Royal Shrovetide Football Match. The ball can be seen in play towards the left of the picture. (Photograph by Andy Savage of www.derbyphotos.co.uk)

6 The parade at the start of the Hare Pie Scramble at Hallaton in Leicestershire, led by a man carrying a pole surmounted by a leaping bronze hare and a woman carrying a basket full of penny loaves. (Courtesy of Biff Raven-Hill, www.wartimehousewife.wordpress.com)

*7 It's behind you! A young straw bear loiters among the crowd at the Whittlesea Straw Bear Festival.
(Courtesy of James Yardley)*

*8 Constable, officials and Tutti-wenches, Hocktide 2004. Mrs Barbara Barr was the first lady Constable
since records began in 1458. (Courtesy of Dr Hugh Pihlens)*

9 Revd Grant Fellows, the rector of All Saints' Church in Leighton Buzzard, is seen upending a choir member outside the almshouses in North Street, during the 2010 Wilkes Walk. Also in the picture are Friar David Teasdel the curate of the parish to the left, the choir, trustees of the almshouse charity and other officials. (Courtesy of Terry Warburton MBE)

10 On Oak Apple Day a small group of women from Great Wishford in Wiltshire dressed in traditional costume perform a dance outside Salisbury Cathedral, which is said to symbolise women who protested when the lord of the manor threatened to take away their right to gather firewood in Grovely Wood. (Courtesy of Ed Scutt)

11 *Green ladies join the procession at the Hastings Traditional Jack in the Green Festival. (Courtesy of Colin Bewes)*

12 *Traditional dancers perform in front of Rochester Cathedral at the Rochester Sweeps Festival during the May Day Bank Holiday weekend. (© Simon Kelsey)*

13 The Sowerby Bridge rushcart is pulled through the lanes between several Yorkshire villages during the annual Rushbearing Festival, which now takes place over the first weekend in September. (Photo courtesy of Sowerby Bridge Rushbearing Association, copyright C. Coe)

14 Six rush maidens carry a special linen sheet containing token rushes during the rushbearing procession at Grasmere. (Courtesy of Ann Bowker)

15 *Ladies from Belper in Derbyshire press petals on to a well dressing for the town's Well Dressing Festival. (Courtesy of Ann Pocklington)*

16 *Ladies of Ye Olde Lewes Borough Bonfire Society in Tudor dress during the Bonfire Night celebrations at Lewes in Sussex. (Courtesy of Lewes Borough Bonfire Society)*

public house in Little Dunmow, who, although having had several unsuccessful marriages, is determined to win the flitch. Ainsworth moves the location of the trials to the Town Hall in Great Dunmow, and it seems that in a master stroke of Victorian publicity for his tome, a flitch trial was organised for 1855, in which Ainsworth was invited to be the judge. I am not certain whether this was the intention of the committee who met to arrange the event and invited the author to participate, but he certainly took full advantage of the situation. The book was an enormous success and the trials were extensively covered in the *Illustrated London News*. The modern-day trials unquestionably date from this time, as Friar Bacon writes:

> The first few years of the Trials after Harrison Ainsworth were conducted without a Jury, but there seemed little point in couples just turning up and claiming the Flitch without being put properly on Trial. The Jury was brought back and since that time it has been a Jury of bachelors and spinsters from Great Dunmow who have determined whether the couples are happily married or not. The Committee who now runs the Flitch Trials has a fairly comprehensive list of the successful claimants of the Flitch Trials, however, there are also records of some losers. There are two delightful prints recording the couple that was successful in claiming the Flitch, but, as they were trying to take it away they discovered the bag was too small and the wife then ranted at the husband about the size of the bag. The Flitch was taken away and shared among all the people present.
>
> In modern times the Flitch has been lost by many a good couple who have fallen foul of the Jury. On one occasion, the husband had explained that his hobby was train spotting and in cross-examination was asked whether he wore a duffle coat or anorak. It was the wife who answered, saying that she would not let him go out looking like that! The bachelors on the Jury obviously felt that she had her poor husband under her thumb. How can you be a true train spotter without either a duffle coat or anorak?

Of course there have also been infallible cases brought before the jury, such as that of the sea captain and his wife, who had not seen each other since the day of their marriage. This was because he had been at sea and had only returned on the day of their trial. And there was the case of the claimant whose wife was dumb – nobody could find any fault with her testimony!

10

HOCKTIDE

ONCE A WIDESPREAD activity, Hocktide now finds itself isolated to the single parish of Hungerford in Berkshire where, although festivities take place over several days, the main event occurs on the second Tuesday after Easter which is known as Tutti-Day, and which coincides with the end of the financial and administrative year. Hocktide as now practised in the town is possibly the merging together of two, or even three earlier customs.

The origins of the word itself are not known, although it possibly derives from the Anglo-Saxon term *heah-tit*, meaning high festival. There is no trace of the word in Old English and its earliest recorded use as Hock-Day comes from the twelfth century, by which time the festivities centred on a practice known as binding, when the men of the parish would tie up the women, demanding a kiss for their release. The following day the ladies would return the indignity, by tying up the menfolk and demanding a monetary payment before setting them free. The monies collected would then be donated to parish funds. As can be imagined, this was accompanied with hearty bouts of drinking. Binding is thought to have been the celebration of one of possibly two important historical events in Saxon chronology, neither of which occurred near Easter, which in itself makes this conjecture highly dubious.

The first of these was the massacre of the Danes on 13 November 1002 by order of King Ethelred the Unready. This was the feast day of St Brice, a fifth-century Bishop of Tours. During the previous decade some parts of England had been ravaged and inhabited by the Danes, and the King believed that they were plotting to murder him and seize his throne. The exact extent of this genocide is a matter of historical debate, but among those thought to have been slain were Pallig Tokesen, a Danish nobleman, who the king had made the Earl of Devonshire, and his wife Gunhilde, the sister of King Sweyn I of Denmark, who was known as Forkbeard.

The second event was the death of Harthacanute on 8 June 1042, which in itself shows that Ethelred's plan to eradicate the Danes in England was unsuccessful. In fact, it only served to encourage further raids on the country in revenge. Harthacanute had already been King of Denmark for five years when he became King of England in 1040. He was said to have been a harsh and cruel monarch of whom the *Anglo-Saxon Chronicle* accuses, 'never accomplished anything kingly for as long as he ruled.' His death was therefore met with great rejoicing.

How either of these events became associated with binding though is anybody's guess, but in Coventry, a pageant emerged out of these celebrations that went under the name of the Old Coventry Play of Hock-Tuesday. This performance is said to have depicted the struggle between the Saxons and the Danes and culminated with the arrival of Saxon women to help their menfolk defeat their enemies and thereafter bind them, before leading them off into captivity.

At the time of the Reformation, Henry VIII suppressed these activities, as he was concerned about the drunken disorder with which they had become associated. However, when his daughter, Queen Elizabeth I, visited Kenilworth in July 1575, somebody had the audacity to put on a performance of the play, much to her apparent amusement. After that, Hocktide appears to have had something of a renaissance, flourishing until the end of the seventeenth century, by which time it had largely fizzled out again.

But other than the kissing aspect of binding, nothing else from this earlier custom seems to bear any relevance to the way that Hocktide is now celebrated in Hungerford, were it not for the mention of Hock-Tuesday, which brings us to the second and third customs to which it is possibly aligned.

In centuries past, Hock-Tuesday was an important calendar event for both peasants and gentry. Along with Michaelmas it divided the rural year into winter and summer, when contracts were renewed between landlords and tenants, and, perhaps more importantly, rents or tithes became payable. Hock-Tuesday heralded the start of the summer term.

Similarly, there were the medieval Tourns, adjudicated by a sheriff at each of the hundreds in his shire. The sheriff was a royal official responsible for keeping the peace on behalf of the king, while hundreds were areas of land over which he administered, mainly for military and judicial purposes, under the common law introduced by the Saxons between 613 and 1017.

Each hundred was large enough to sustain a hundred households headed by a hundred-man. The hundreds were themselves divided into tithings containing ten households, while the basic unit of land supporting a single family was called a hide.

Within each hundred there was a meeting house where, roughly once every three weeks, the men gathered to hold a hundred-court in which they decided the penalties awarded to minor offenders. But at Easter and Michaelmas the sheriff would visit each of the hundreds in his shire to hold a criminal court, known as the Tourn.

Everyone who had freehold land was expected to attend this court and would be fined if they did not. By the thirteenth century these Tourns had become well established over much of the land. Presently you will observe the striking similarity between these historic proceedings, Hock-Tuesday, and the way that Hocktide is now observed in Hungerford.

But why does Hocktide now survive only in Hungerford? In 1362, the manor of Hungerford passed to John of Gaunt (1340-1399), the first Duke of Lancaster, who granted grazing rights to the townsfolk, along with permission to fish in the River Kennet. Later, during the reign of Queen Elizabeth I (1558-1603), the Duchy of Lancaster tried to reclaim these lucrative fishing rights, but the commoners stood their ground, which led to a lengthy legal wrangle that in the end was decided by Good Queen Bess herself, who interceded on the side of the commoners. In celebration of this victory, Hocktide in Hungerford now perhaps combines the ceremonial collection of rents on Hock-Tuesday, with elements of the Tourns and the custom of demanding kisses or money.

Before the annual celebrations can begin a number of officials have to be in place, who are an integral part of the Tutti-Day proceedings. Some of these might have held their office for many years. They include the Constable, the Orange man, Tutti-wenches, and Tutti-men or tithing men, applications for which are no doubt plentiful as they get to do some of the kissing.

Also needed is a Tutti Jury, the twelve members of which are normally confirmed during a special meeting at the Town Hall about a week beforehand, although they might already have been decided upon at the Macaroni Supper, which takes place on the Friday of Easter week at the John of Gaunt Inn. Here, the Constable and other serving officers of the Hocktide Court enjoy a feast of macaroni cheese and watercress while discussing suitable candidates for positions within the new court and its associated ceremony.

At the subsequent meeting in the Town Hall the attendance of all commoners is expected. Those who are chosen to sit on the jury will be issued with a summons as jurors to attend the Hocktide Court the following Tuesday.

Tutti-men visit Hungerford Workhouse during Hocktide in 1913. (Courtesy of Dr Hugh Pihlens)

On the Monday evening before Tutti-Day, an ale-tasting unfolds in the Corn Exchange. This is a fairly recent addition to the festival, during which the Constable and the official ale-tasters sample various pints and consume a cold buffet, all of which helps fuel their enthusiasm for the following morning and the start of that year's main event.

At eight o'clock on the morning of Tutti-Day itself, the town crier, or Bellman as he is known, summons all commoners to attend the Hocktide Court from the balcony of the Town Hall by blowing the Constable's Horn. This horn was presented in 1992 to replace the Lucas Horn of 1634, which was then considered far too old and precious for regular use. The Lucas Horn had itself replaced the even earlier John of Gaunt Horn, which may actually date from the fifteenth century. The Bellman, who is also the assistant bailiff and beadle, then shouts the following proclamation:

> Oyez! Oyez! All ye commoners of the town and manor of Hungerford are requested to attend your court house at nine o'clock this morning on pain of being fined. God save the Queen!

He then repeats the summons a number of times more, while negotiating the length and breadth of both the High Street and Bridge Street.

By 9 a.m. all have gathered at the Town Hall steps, where the Constable presents the Tutti-men with their Tutti poles. These are wooden staffs decorated with ribbons and topped with bunches of spring flowers and a cloven orange. They are thought to have derived from nosegays, or posies, made of sweet-smelling flowers which, in times past, could have counteracted some of the unpleasant odours experienced in the less prosperous corners of the town. Tutti-Day almost certainly derives its name from these poles, as a 'Tutti' is a West Country term for a nosegay.

Accompanied by the Orange man and the Tutti-wenches, the Tutti-men set off to collect the dues owed by those dwelling in common right properties. They visit each in turn, of which there are roughly a hundred. In former times they collected the Hock-Tuesday rents, while now they merely demand a penny or a kiss from the lady of the household and or a penny from the gentleman of the abode. They might also accept a little hospitality along the way. In return they give out oranges, which the Orange man draws out of a large white sack which he carries. The Orange man, who is a sort of mentor to the Tutti-men, having served as one himself for many years, traditionally wears a top hat festooned with feathers.

While all of this is going on, other commoners attend the Hocktide Court in the Town Hall, which commences at 9.05 a.m. Similar to the sheriff in the ancient Tourns, the Constable heads the court and does so from a carved ebony chair of Elizabethan origin, which is known as the John of Gaunt chair. The Lucas Horn is laid in front of him before the session can begin.

Next, the Hocktide Jury is sworn in and elects their foreman. The roll of commoners is called and any who are absent will be fined or lose their grazing and fishing rights for the coming year. Of course, some of those absent will be at home waiting for the Tutti-men to drop by, in which case they elect a friend to pay their fine for them.

Other business during the Hocktide Court includes the reading of the ancient customs by the steward of the manor, which have been handed down through the ages. The accounts are read and agreed, officers are elected for the coming year and other matters relating to the town and manor are discussed.

From around 1 p.m. the Hocktide Jury, commoners and their guests then enjoy a Hocktide luncheon at the Corn Exchange, at which the traditional Plantagenet Punch is served. This is another reference to John of Gaunt, who was a member of the Plantagenet dynasty and third surviving son of Edward III. During this luncheon and using the large pewter tankards that symbolise their office, the Ale-Tasters judge the quality of the ale being served.

After the meal an initiation ceremony known as 'shoeing the colts' is held, in which all first-time attendees are shod by the blacksmith. Their legs are held and a nail driven into their shoe. They are not released until they shout 'Punch!'

The Constable (seated) with the Bellman and the Tutti-men holding their Tutti-poles, during Hocktide in 1910. (Courtesy of Dr Hugh Pihlens)

Shoeing the Colts during Hocktide 1913 in the courtyard of The Three Swans Hotel. More recently this takes place in the Corn Exchange. (Courtesy of Dr Hugh Pihlens)

Although this might seem a little dangerous, it is carried out light-heartedly and without causing injury.

Other associated activities continue around the town for several more days before the curtain finally closes on another Hocktide and one of the most important dates in Hungerford's calendar, not to mention a thriving link to England's ancient past.

Having digested all of this, one obvious question remains, why are oranges so prevalent in this particular custom? It is probably due to the fact that similar to John of Gaunt, Prince William of Orange was another historical figure associated with the town. For it was here on 6 December 1688 that he met with the commissioners of King James II at the Bear Inn, after he had landed at Brixham in Devon and marched on London with his army. Talks ensued which ultimately paved the way for the crown of England to pass from James to William and, in so doing, from the Stuart line to the Hanoverians. William III reigned from 1689 to 1702, at first jointly with his wife, together known as William and Mary.

11

BEATING THE BOUNDS

A WIDESPREAD CUSTOM in former times with an eccle-siastical bent was 'beating the bounds', during which a priest accompanied by church wardens and choristers would walk around the boundary of their parish followed by the villagers. At various points along the route the priest would pray that no harm would befall his community during the approaching year and that their crops would be plentiful. Boundary markers at these locations would then be ritually beaten with sticks. In some places these rituals were known as 'riding the marches', 'riding the fringes', or just 'common riding'. Similar ceremonies were also known to the Anglo-Saxons and Vikings as 'Gang Days' and occurred at Rogationtide. '*Gangen*' was the Norse term for 'to walk'.

There are four Rogation Days in the Christian calendar, the first of which, known as the Major Rogation, coincided with St Mark's Day on 25 April, although the saint in question had absolutely nothing to do with the ceremony – it is just a coincidence. The Minor Rogations apply to the three days prior to Ascension Day, which is observed itself on Holy Thursday during the fifth week after Easter, making them Rogation Monday, Tuesday and Wednesday. Traditionally, these four dates were celebrated with solemn processions designed to invoke God's mercy.

These ceremonies could have derived from several sources, including an ancient Roman festival called Robigalia, likewise observed on 25 April, which also involved processions, prayers and sacrifices to the gods in the hope of reaping a bounteous harvest. With the emergence of Christianity, the festival was adopted and customised for the new religious order. The Major Rogation was also known as the Greater Litanies and if it coincided with Easter it would be moved to the 27 April instead. But there are also similarities with the pagan festival of

Beltane, in which birch twigs or besoms were struck against boundary markers, thus pre-dating the Roman occupation of these lands.

The Minor Rogations or Lesser Litanies on the other hand, were said to have been inaugurated by St Mamertus around AD 470, who at the time was the Archbishop of Vienne in Gaul, and thereafter spread to other Christian enclaves of the world including Britain where they were observed with fasting. It also became common for farmers at this time of year to have their crops blessed by the local rector. So perhaps the act of beating the bounds evolved from one or several of these older customs.

But why were boundaries considered important enough to warrant such attention? Before the days of Ordnance Survey maps, or indeed any sort of formal map, it was crucial for people to be aware of farm, manorial, church or civil boundaries. In feudal England, land was everything and it was important to know not only the extent of your own community but that of your neighbours. In earlier times tribal boundaries would have been equally significant, while similarly in the medieval world, understanding the position of one's boundary was vital to preventing neighbouring groups encroaching beyond it. It also had economic relevance in defining common rights to things like grazing pasture and firewood collection. As can be imagined, boundary disputes were common and sometimes resulted in bloodshed.

Natural features such as large rocks, rivers or isolated trees were often designated as boundary markers and adolescents were expected to know their whereabouts. Sometimes walls, hedges or other man-made features were also used, including specially placed boundary stones, or even stone crosses.

Boundaries were particularly important to the Church, which claimed entitlement to a tithe of all produce gathered in the parish. This amounted to one tenth of everything, so the position of a boundary would determine the value of this tithe and was therefore of great significance to the wealth of the clergy.

In time processions evolved in many parts of the country, no doubt echoing the earlier Roman or pagan customs, in which a horde of people, both young and old, would perambulate their boundary behind the local priest, who would preach and give a blessing at the various markers along the route. Such processions would typically occur once every seven or ten years. At one time they are known to have been very colourful, with participants carrying banners depicting the saints and chanting from the scriptures. Often, when two adjoining parishes held ceremonies at the same time, the processions might encounter one another somewhere along the line and simmering disputes could boil over. At the time of the Commonwealth, Oliver Cromwell banned these ceremonies as well as the parading of colourful banners.

In some communities, elm, birch or willow wands were used to 'beat' the boundary markers. The bark was first removed, exposing the white wood beneath. Such dramatic interludes were designed to firmly cement the location of the marker into the memory of those present, particularly younger members of the throng.

At one time there was also a legal side to these proceedings, as beating the bounds helped to reinforce royal and baronial charters. These were documents that recorded the rights of the ruling and wealthier classes, over property and people. So in medieval days the ceremonial processing around their land served to reinforce the power and influence that the holder of the charter had over their tenants and serfs. Regular perambulation, at least once every seven to ten years, ensured that each succeeding generation understood their place in the overall scheme of things, and to whom they owed their allegiance. In England at least, it appears that beating the bounds was a coming together of both these legal and parochial ceremonies. In time, as the jurisdiction of the manorial estates was succeeded by the Church, it became almost entirely associated with the latter.

One place where a descendant form of the custom still survives, albeit with an unusual twist, is Leighton Buzzard in Bedfordshire. Here it is known as the Wilkes Walk and includes an eccentricity called 'upending'.

In the seventeenth century a gentleman called Edward Wilkes was a great benefactor to the town and in 1630 built almshouses in North Street in memory of his late father, John, which are still there to this day. He also established a trust fund to help pay for the accommodation of the poor and needy of the parish, which also continues to the present.

One of Edward's sons, Matthew Wilkes, wanted his father's generosity to be remembered and the Wilkes Walk originated from a provision in his will, which called for an annual procession to take place led by a garland bearer and involving the clergy, choir and church wardens of All Saints' Church, together with the trustees of the Wilkes charity.

This procession, which takes place on Rogation Monday (the Monday before Ascension Day), begins at All Saints' Church at around 11.45 a.m. and winds its way through the town to the almshouses, where a short service is held before moving on to the market cross. However, this in itself wasn't thought-provoking enough for Matthew Wilkes, who wanted the occasion to be unique in order for people to remember it. So, during the annual recital of an extract from Edward's will by the clerk, Matthew decreed that a choirboy should be upended in front of the almshouses, or, in other words, dangled upside down by his ankles, for which he would be rewarded with the princely sum of five shillings. All the other members of the choir received two shillings and sixpence.

The Wilkes Walk procession makes its way through the town of Leighton Buzzard. (Courtesy of Terry Warburton, MBE)

According to the terms of Matthew's will, as long as this tradition was upheld, the residents of the almshouses and the vicar would be given ten shillings each for their participation. In the seventeenth century this was a significant sum of money and certainly a good motivator, although today the occasion is kept alive for its tradition rather than any financial gain.

After the modern ceremony the whole choir is treated to buns and lemonade back at the church. In former times it would have been buns and beer at the market cross. However, this was stopped in 1896 when large quantities of ale were consumed by these angelic rascals and hundreds, if not thousands of buns were reputedly eaten. The poor ladies of the parish could not keep up with the baking. Even though the tradition of eating the buns at the market cross was later revived, certainly in the last few years this part of the ceremony returns to All Saints, partly because of the weather and partly due to the logistics of moving food from the church to the market cross.

Originally only boys were upended, but today it is just as likely to be a girl. A cushion is now placed strategically beneath their skull just in case they are dropped. Upending itself was not entirely the invention of Matthew Wilkes. In the wider context of beating the bounds, at certain points on the boundary during the navigation, young boys were held upside down and had their heads bumped on the marker stones, the idea being that the pain would help them to remember the location of said markers. Other boys and girls were known to have been beaten with the willow wands, swung violently against markers, or subjected to other unpleasantries. Some would have their backsides ritually caned or birched over or up against the boundary marker.

Beating the bounds in its most traditional format, minus the brutality, can still be observed in a number of places, including Cholesbury and St Leonards in Buckinghamshire. In April 1974, a ceremony occurred here to celebrate the fiftieth anniversary of the creation of the parish. Subsequent beatings have taken place in April 1984 and April 1994. No doubt future ceremonies are also scheduled.

One place where you can definitely still experience this event on a regular basis is at Portland in Dorset, where a special boundary marker can be found on Chesil Beach, about 4 miles to the west of the island. This slab, presumably made of Portland stone, is engraved with the words 'Portland Bound Stone' and marks the northern boundary of the Royal Manor of Portland. A ceremony is held here on Ascension Day once every seven years, during which the islanders re-establish their boundaries by ceremoniously beating two senior pupils from the Royal Manor School. The party is ferried to the spot along the Fleet by a small flotilla of boats and, after making their way to the marker, those who are to be beaten lean over the stone, where they are gently tapped with a reeve staff. The Borough Reeve was a legal figure in past times who carried the staff while collecting rents. The Portland staff is said to be one of the oldest in existence. During the ceremony no blood is spilled or skin bruised and the party returns to the island by the same boats in which they arrived.

Surprisingly, ceremonies of this nature are not confined solely to rural back-waters. For instance, one of the most celebrated events takes place at the Tower of London every third Ascension Day. The procession here is acted out in order to preserve the Tower's boundaries, which are the subject of a centuries-old dispute with its neighbours. The land in question lies outside of the fortifications but has always been considered to be part of the castle complex, and therefore

Crown property and vital to its security. Another purpose of this particular beating is to initiate the children of families connected with the building into its history and traditions.

After meeting on Tower Green on the evening of Ascension Day, the party begins the perambulation of the fortress walls led by the resident governor. Also in attendance will be a number of Yeoman Warders, or 'Beefeaters' as they are more popularly known. The children will be given white wands before setting off.

The company will then proceed around the edges of the Tower of London Liberties and whip the iron plague markers which constitute the outline. In fact, at each successive marker the Tower Chaplain will be heard to shout 'Cursed is he who removeth his neighbour's landmark'. The Chief Warder then commands the youngsters to 'Whack it, boys, whack it', which they do with great enthusiasm using their wands, thus instilling the location of the markers into their memories. No doubt their own descendants will be similarly initiated in the decades ahead.

One of the country's best-supported events occurs annually in Oxford, where visitors each Ascension Day might encounter the sight of several dozen people roaming around the streets armed with stripped willow wands. The processional route here forms the boundary of three parishes, two of which, St Michael at the North Gate and the University Church of St Mary the Virgin, still perform in the traditional way. Both ceremonies kick off with short services, the event at St Michael's starting at 9 a.m. with Holy Communion. This church is notable for its Anglo-Saxon tower dating from 1050, making it the oldest building in the city. All are welcome to attend, whether locals or tourists, and you are just as likely to see a group of camera-toting Japanese or American sightseers in the congregation as students from one of the famous colleges. St Michael's itself can be found at a place called North Gate, where there was once an entrance into the walled city.

Following the service, the worshippers line up outside the church and take their canes from an enormous bundle. The company then starts its walk around the city, visiting various marker stones in turn, which they beat with these sticks. Traditionally, the participants wear dress of office, presuming they have one: the mayor, for instance, wears his gold chain, university members don academic regalia, Boy Scouts their caps and woggles, choristers their bright red surplices etc.

The vicar, who holds a large silver and gold crucifix, marks each stone with a chalk cross and the letters SMNG. He then recites the words 'St Michael at the North Gate' along with the year in question. After this he smartly moves aside

Eight-year-old choirboy Alfie Lay is upended during the 2010 Wilkes Walk in Leighton Buzzard. (Courtesy of Terry Warburton, MBE)

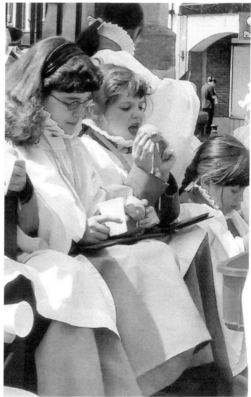

Buns and lemonade on the steps of the market cross in 2004. In the last few years this part of the Wilkes Walk ceremony has been moved to the church, partly because of the weather and partly because of the logistics of moving the food from the church. (Courtesy of Terry Warburton MBE)

as the crowd commences to thrash the markers while shouting 'mark, mark, mark!' Once choirboys were thrashed as well, a practice no longer observed.

The first stone is laid in a wall near Boots the Chemist in Cornmarket Street, the next inside the nearby Littlewoods store, another in Marks and Spencer in Queen Street, and so on. The procession cuts through many shops, public places and historic sites as it climbs fences and descends back streets, for although the boundaries have not changed, the topography has. Both processions pass through Braesenose College at one point. Shoppers and tourists must be bemused by the spectacle, as some of the beaters can get quite animated while letting off steam, often breaking their canes in the process. The final two stones are at Lincoln College, where a free ploughman's lunch is served in the Hall for hungry participants, washed down with ivy beer.

Today, beating the bounds ceremonies can be found in towns and villages across England. Some are staged on a regular basis, while others are held to mark anniversaries or special occasions, such as jubilees or the new millennium.

12

TREE DRESSING

TREE DECORATING AND other arboreal festivals also have varied and ancient roots. Some examples of tree dressing in England are unquestionably pre-Christian and date back thousands of years to a time when Druids would have celebrated the life-giving properties of the forest, and, similar to many other customs, would have been revitalised for the Christian palate. For many centuries the pastoral shepherds living in the hills of the Clun Forest in Shropshire for instance, around the village of Aston-on-Clun, are claimed to have decorated a tree that was well placed at the head of several valleys. In doing so, they believed that the Celtic goddess Brigid would guarantee fertility. After the coming of the Christians and their realisation that in order to convert local people they would have to adopt some of their own deities, Brigid was made a saint.

Other practices trace their beginnings to the long-abolished holiday that was known as Oak Apple Day. This was held every year on 29 May, the birthday of King Charles II. It was also the date on which England became merry again, following years of social repression during Oliver Cromwell's puritanical Commonwealth.

After the English Civil War and the beheading of Charles I in 1649, his son and heir, also called Charles, became an exile in France. When he was twenty-one, the prince sailed to Scotland and was proclaimed king at Scone on 1 January 1651. This did not go down particularly well with the English and when, later that same year he marched across the border heading for the royalist stronghold of the West Midlands at the head of a Scottish army, few Englishmen rallied to his cause. Charles had made a serious error of judgement and at the Battle of Worcester on 3 September he was heavily outnumbered and decisively beaten by Cromwell's New Model Army.

Charles escaped the battlefield and his subsequent evasion of the Roundheads has become the stuff of legends. Across the country there are places that lay claim to harbouring the fugitive prince during this desperate flight. Paramount among these is Boscobel Hall in Staffordshire, where Charles is claimed to have hidden in the branches of an oak tree in the grounds of the house, while Cromwell's cohorts searched below. This tree, known as the Boscobel Oak, is also responsible for giving hundreds, if not thousands of public houses their name, The Royal Oak, as well as several ships of the Royal Navy.

By the early 1700s, over-zealous monarchist souvenir hunters had literally hacked the tree to death, branch by branch. However, one of its acorns sprouted into a new tree beside it, which is the Royal Oak that can still be seen today, known as Son of Royal Oak. And it now has a grandson, as in 2001, to mark the 350th anniversary of the escape of his ancestor, Prince Charles planted a sapling nearby that was grown from one of the son's acorns.

Following the death of Oliver Cromwell in 1658 and the collapse of the republic, Charles returned again in May 1660, and this time successfully restored the monarchy to become King Charles II. At the same time he declared a general amnesty for all those who had fought against him and his father, or had adverse political views. The restoration promised to heal the divisions that had plagued the land for so long and brought a new era of enlightenment, which earned Charles the nickname, the Merry Monarch. The 29th of May 1660 was not only the king's thirtieth birthday but the date on which he entered London and acceded the throne, although he was not actually crowned King of Great Britain and Ireland until 23 April 1661. Four years after his ascension, Parliament decreed that from that day forth 29 May would be kept as a public holiday, to be known as Oak Apple Day.

Around the realm this new holiday manifested itself in many different ways. Some communities adapted ancient customs that already existed to coincide with it. In many places trees were dressed with flags and there was feasting, drinking and dancing. People celebrated to excess, relieved by the lifting of the grey veil of Puritan austerity. To openly celebrate any form of ancient festival during the Commonwealth was extremely dangerous, so for ordinary rural people this was a hugely important event, the significance of which is hard for us to appreciate in today's relatively free society.

It became the custom to wear a sprig of oak on Oak Apple Day, as a symbol of your loyalty to the restored king. Those who refused ran the risk of being set upon in the street and physically abused; at the very least having mud thrown at them. Children were also encouraged to become involved and would challenge each other to show their sprig. The penalty for failing to do so was to

Oak Apple Day procession in the Dorset village of Stourton Caundle, 29 May 1922. (Courtesy of Phil Knott)

have your bottom pinched. Consequently, among juveniles taking part in the practice, which continued in some places until quite recent times, it became known as Pinch-Bum Day. The children would also chant the rhyme, 'The 29th of May is Oak Apple Day. If you don't give us a holiday, we'll all run away.' In some parts of England the festival was also known as Shick-Shack Day, the explanations for which are again varied, but the most commonly quoted being that a shick-shack was once another term for an oak apple in some areas. Others suggest it was a term of abuse and calling someone a shick-shack might have been rather unpleasant.

Even though Oak Apple Day was abolished in 1859, some communities refused to let it die. Today, several places still observe a form of tree dressing that can be traced back to this lamented and very English celebration. In the village of Great Wishford for instance, near Wilton in Wiltshire, 29 May is still a special day in the calendar. On this day the people of the village perpetuate their ancient right to collect firewood in nearby Grovely Wood. This practice pre-dates the restoration and in fact goes right back to 1292, when the villagers first legally protected their wood rights at court, so in itself it is another good example of how ancient customs have become interwoven with new.

Traditionally, at first light on festival day, the men from the village make their way to the forest where oak boughs are removed, which must include an oak apple. One of these is then decorated and later in the day a procession bears it to St Giles' Church, where it is hung from the tower. While all of this is going on the women of the village would decorate their cottages with flags and bunting. In order to maintain their charter, the villagers must proclaim their right at a special ceremony in Salisbury Cathedral. Here a small group of women dressed in traditional costume perform a dance in the cathedral close, which is said to symbolise women who protested when the lord of the manor threatened to take away their right to gather the wood. At many times during the history of the village landowners have attempted to thwart the custom, eager to use the forest for hunting. Following the dance, the villagers repeat the ancient refrain, shouted at full volume, 'Grovely, Grovely, and all Grovely'. Very poetic were the ancestors of Great Wishford. The celebrations are then continued back at the village with a dinner, dancing, general revelry and even a fair, all of which is organised by the Oak Apple Club.

In Aston-on-Clun the people also chose to adapt their ancient tree dressing festival to make it coincide with Oak Apple Day, and here it became known as Arbor Day, which is now held on the last Sunday in May. This was certainly not the only place where Arbor Day was observed, but it is now the custom's only remaining vestige. Arbor Day became a hugely popular ceremony and each year the Arbor Tree, which was a black poplar situated within the confines of the village, would be dressed in gaily-coloured flags and there would be much merriment. For a hundred years or more this tradition was upheld at various levels of interest, when in 1786, the long-term survival of the custom at Aston-on-Clun was secured, while in other places it slowly faded away. The reason for this was that a local squire called John Marston, on arriving back in the village after his wedding to Mary Carter of Sibdon Castle and full of nuptial bliss, was so inspired by the joy of the celebrations taking place that he set up a trust fund to pay for the care of the tree and flags. Remarkably, the money he provided lasted right up until the mid-1950s, when Hopesay Parish Council took up the gauntlet to continue his bequest.

Since the time of Squire Marston the Arbor Day festival has seen many ups and downs in its fortunes. Although the original tree, which was over 300 years old, was blown down in a storm in 1995 and was replaced by a twenty-year-old sapling, the tree dressing festival still continues each year. In the 1950s, it evolved into an annual wedding pageant when children dressed up in the clothes worn in the days of Squire Marston and his blushing bride. There is now a colourful procession, headed by children dressed as the bride and groom, the vicar and villagers of old. There is also an associated day of fun and games, as well as performances around the tree. But it was not until the Queen's Silver

The Arbor Tree at Aston-on-Clun in Shropshire, pictured in 1911. The tree is shown decorated with flags and buntings. (Courtesy of Rosie Evans)

Jubilee year of 1977 that the wedding pageant was truly revitalised and since then the festival has thrived, going from strength to strength.

Another celebration on Oak Apple Day takes place at All Saints' Church in Northampton, where a wreath is put around a statue of King Charles II. All Saints' Church, or All Hallows as it is sometimes known, was largely destroyed in the great fire of Northampton in 1675 and rebuilt using timber donated from the royal forests of Selcey and Rockingham. During the Civil War, Northampton had been staunchly Parliamentarian, but the King's magnanimous gesture, together with the repeal of the chimney tax, so endeared him to the people of the town, that as a result a statue by John Hunt was erected in the portico parapet in 1712. For some reason he is wearing a Roman toga and armour. Underneath the statue is the following text:

> This statue was erected in memory of King Charles II who gave a thousand tun of timber towards the rebuilding of this church and to this town seven years chimney money collected in it.

One of the strangest customs associated with Oak Apple Day is the procession of the Garland King and Queen at Castleton in Derbyshire, which has absolutely nothing to do with the restoration of the monarchy. Castleton owes

The Garland King and his consort during Castleton Garland Day 1976. (© Simon Garbutt)

its name to Peveril Castle, a Norman keep which overlooks it, that was once the seat of William Peveril, bailiff of the Royal Manors of the Peak District after the Norman Conquest. It is suggested that Peveril was one of William the Conqueror's illegitimate sons. One rather suspects that when he first took up residence in the area, the Garland King might already have been an established fixture. During the Commonwealth the procession was outlawed, but as soon as Charles restored the throne and offered amnesty, once again the Garland King began to ride through the streets of Castleton, now dressed in the costume of a seventeenth-century gentleman, and conveniently parading on Oak Apple Day.

Every year on 29 May the Garland King rides through the streets of the village on his horse, at the head of a procession. His head and the upper part of his body are completely hidden beneath the garland. This is a heavy wooden structure shaped like a cone, festooned with wild flowers and greenery. The whole thing can weigh between 25–30kg, so the king's task is quite arduous. On top of the garland is a small posy of flowers called the Queen Posy.

Behind the king in the procession rides his queen. In former times her part was played by a man dressed in woman's clothing but now a female performs the role. All the while they are accompanied by children performing country dances and a band playing music. The royal couple parade slowly around the village, stopping at every pub, of which there are several, with names like Ye Olde Cheshire Cheese Inn, Ye Olde Nag's Head, and the Castle Hotel.

Eventually the parade arrives at the village square and the garland is hoisted up to the top of St Edmund's Church tower and fixed to one of its eight pinnacles, where it will remain for the coming months. The Queen Posy is then placed on the village war memorial, and there is morris dancing and music around the garland maypole.

Among other places that still have traditions associated with Oak Apple Day are Upton-upon-Severn in Worcestershire, Marsh Gibbon in Buckinghamshire, and Membury in Devon. At the Royal Hospital in Chelsea, which was founded by Charles II, it is traditional to drink beer and eat plum pudding. At some halls at both Oxford and Cambridge, a toast is drunk to celebrate the Merry Monarch. And even now traditional royalists decorate their houses with oak branches or even wear a sprig of oak.

At Appleton Thorn in Cheshire another annual tree dressing ceremony is known as Bawming the Thorn, which is held on the third Saturday in June, this being the nearest Saturday to Midsummer's Day. The hawthorn tree in question stands in the middle of the village near the Church of St Cross, which was built in 1886. The tree is claimed to be a descendant of the more famous

Glastonbury Holy Thorn, a cutting of which was brought to Appleton by local landowner and crusading knight, Adam de Dutton.

In regards to the Glastonbury Thorn, it is said that Jesus Christ had a great-uncle known as Joseph of Arimathea. Joseph was a merchant and his ships often came to England in search of tin. Legend has it that on one journey, Joseph came to Glastonbury in Somerset, which at that time was an island rising out of the marshes, the Isle of Glass (Ynys Witrin), later known as the Isle of Avalon, which would become central to the stories of King Arthur and the quest for the Holy Grail. On one particular trip, Joseph was accompanied by the young Jesus, who was employed as a ship's carpenter. Jesus would undoubtedly have trained to be a carpenter, as the tradition was always to follow in your father's footsteps. We know very little about Jesus, until he was around thirty, which was an entire lifetime in those distant days. Indeed, the same legend is also told in the Maronite villages of Galilee, where many people today still believe that Jesus came to Britain, remaining for much of the winter because of bad weather. And during that winter he helped Joseph to build a simple place of worship out of the twisted English wattles, to administer to the spiritual needs of the sailors. Perhaps the best-known champion of this legend was William Blake, who in his hymn 'Jerusalem' asks the question: 'And did those feet in ancient time, walk upon England's mountains green? And was the holy Lamb of God on England's pleasant pastures seen?'

As well as being a merchant Joseph was a very important man, a member of the Sanhedrin, the highest Jewish council of justice. He was also a secret follower of Christ and on the day of the crucifixion, he provided a sepulchre for the Lord's body. When Jesus was taken down from the cross, Joseph plucked one of the thorns from the crown of thorns that the Roman soldiers had placed on his head. Legend has it that a staff grew from the thorn. Joseph thereafter took the staff and travelled around the world, spreading Christianity. He also took with him the Holy Grail, which was the chalice used by Jesus and his disciples at the Last Supper, and a pair of cruets containing Christ's sweat and blood. When Joseph returned to England, near the spot where Christ had earlier helped him build a chapel, he thrust the staff into the ground and sighed, 'Now we are weary all'. Miraculously, the staff took root and grew into a thorn tree. The place is still called Wearyall Hill and nearby Joseph built the first Christian church in England, on the spot where Glastonbury Abbey stands today.

There are now several Holy Thorns around Glastonbury and the one on Wearyall Hill is said to be a direct descendent from the one that sprouted from Joseph's staff. It still survives, in spite of being subjected to a brutal act of vandalism in December 2010. Sprigs from one in St John the Baptist churchyard are cut each December to send to the Queen's Christmas table. In 2011, an extra sprig was sent in April to Prince William and Kate Middleton on the occasion of their marriage.

At one time Appleton Thorn was a small community of scattered cottages and it wasn't until the nineteenth century that it took on any significance, with the building of the church and the old school, which is now the village hall. It is from here that a parade sets out on Bawming Day at 12.45 p.m. to arrive at the tree by 1 p.m., where children dance and sing the Bawming Song, which includes the following chorus:

> Up with fresh garlands this Midsummer morn,
> Up with red ribbons on Appleton Thorn.
> Come lasses and lads to the Thorn Tree today,
> To Bawn it and shout as ye Bawm it, Hooray!

It is not known how old this ceremony is, although the current practice dates from the nineteenth century, when it was part of the village's walking day. At that time it involved children from Appleton Thorn Primary School walking through the village, before holding sports and games at the school. The ceremony was stopped in the 1930s but was later revived by the then headmaster, Mr Bob Jones, in 1967.

Andrew Bain, vice chairman of the Bawming Committee, explains that although in theory the local children are expected to decorate the tree, in practise it is mostly done by members of the committee themselves, all of whom are volunteers. The actual bawming of the tree is done with red ribbons to tie in with the song. This takes place about a week before the celebration. These ribbons are usually renewed every two or three years. As well as the bawming ceremony itself, the celebrations include children's sports at the village hall and a fête.

So, tree dressing days and festivals are still common fixtures in the rural calendars of some parts of the country. Perhaps one of the best known takes place at the Weald and Downland Open Air Museum at Singleton, near Chichester in West Sussex. The aim of the museum has always been to keep alive the traditions of our rural past for future generations to appreciate, and the annual tree dressing event is a fine example of this. It is a fascinating and unusual celebration for all the family. As darkness descends the finale of the day is an enchanting procession and spiral dance around two magnificent aspen trees, which are dressed with hundreds of lanterns that have been made during the afternoon.

Colourful lanterns dress the aspen trees, as dusk settles on the tree dressing event at the Weald and Downland Open Air Museum, near Chichester, West Sussex. (Courtesy of The Weald and Downland Open Air Museum)

With its origins in the green man legends and other ancient customs celebrating the life-giving properties of trees and the natural world, this event enables visitors to both enjoy and join in traditional songs, dances, plays and stories about trees and the countryside. Visitors of all ages, but mainly children, are invited to make a lantern during the afternoon at a museum workshop. These are then lit for the final procession. The lanterns are then hung in the aspen trees and make a spectacular display of colour and light.

Without question, the most popular form of tree dressing is of course Christmas, but the joy of decorating Christmas trees as practised in England today has little to do with any of our native ancestral folk customs. In fact, it has more to do with German folklore. Saint Boniface is credited with inventing the custom, when, during his mission to convert pagan tribes away from their old gods, he chopped down the Oak of Thor at Geismar, only to discover a tiny fir tree growing among its roots. This was a sign from God, he claimed, and the heathens succumbed, after which the fir tree became an emblem of Christianity in Germany. By the sixteenth century Christmas trees were widespread throughout that country, with Martin Luther (1483-1546) reputedly adding the first lights. Perhaps the oldest known official source of a decorated Christmas tree comes from the records of Strasbourg cathedral in 1539.

Being of Hanoverian descent, in England Christmas trees were enjoyed by the monarchy long before entering the public domain. The thirteen-year-old princess Victoria wrote about Christmas trees hung with lights and sugar ornaments, under which presents were placed, in her journal of 1832. But it was really a woodcut of the happy royal family around their tree at Osborne House published in the *Illustrated London News* in December 1848 that catapulted the tradition into popular culture. Whatever the royal couple did would be eagerly copied by the affluent of society and a tradition was born.

So in modern Britain there are still many examples of tree dressing, some quite ancient and others very modern. Some are celebrated in the spring as a fertility rite, while others are celebrated in the winter to add colour and body to deciduous trees that have lost their summer foliage. From pagan Druids to Christian priests, the decorating of trees are symbols of our country's varied and evolving beliefs.

13

JACK IN THE GREEN

A JACK IN the Green was once a traditional component of many May Day parades, now relegated to a handful of revivals. In this custom the tables are turned, as instead of a tree being decorated, a man adopts an arboreal disguise similar to Castleton's Garland King but on a much grander scale.

The Jack is a large framework structure swathed in lush green foliage and spring flowers, which is sometimes surmounted by an elaborate floral crown and then worn or carried by a person – who is completely hidden by the leaves and has their face painted green. These Jacks can be anything up to 9ft tall and were intended to give the illusion that a bush or small tree had developed a life of its own, in the human understanding of the word.

Although this smacks of paganism, the custom's origin might only date from the sixteenth century, when people created intricate garlands of flowers and leaves to carry during their local May Day processions. Milkmaids, for instance, were said to carry garlands on their heads strewn with polished silverware. They would support utensils piled up like a pyramid, comprising such things as silver cups, pots and spoons, which must have weighed a ton. By the eighteenth century the all-enveloping structure, now known as the Jack, had begun to make an appearance and, reputedly, was introduced by chimney sweeps, who were determined to net as much income from these parades as possible during what was traditionally a quiet time of year for their business.

The earliest known record of a Jack in the Green comes from an edition of *The Times* from 4 May 1785, when an example made an appearance before the Prince of Wales during a pageant in Oxford. Although the practice had almost died out by the nineteenth century, it has now

Jack in the Green is a large framework structure swathed in vegetation, which is then worn by a person completely concealed by the greenery. (Courtesy of Mad Jack's Morris)

been revived in a number of places. May Day parades at the time in question were apparently quite raucous and two further characters regularly taking part in these processions were the Lord and Lady of the May, renowned for their practical-joking. Jack would interact with these and all of them became labelled for their drunkenness and debauchery.

During the nineteenth century and the advent of a more prim and proper society, May Day celebrations underwent a radical shake-up to appease Victorian stuffiness. The bawdiness of the Lord and Lady of the May was no longer tolerated and, instead, a pretty young May Queen graced the parade, bringing serenity where previously clamour had existed. Likewise, there was no longer a role in these proceedings for poor Jack with his drunken tomfoolery and slowly the custom expired. Another nail in Jack's personal coffin was the passing of the Climbing Boys' Act in 1868, which outlawed the practice of sending boys up chimney breasts.

Matthew Alexander, a member of Pilgrim Morris Men who parade a revived Jack in Guildford known as the 'Guildford Bush', reveals the history of the practice in this area of Surrey:

The recorded history of Guildford's Jack in the Green stretches all the way back to 1976, when the Pilgrim Morris Men revived the 'Summerpole' traditions. The inclusion of the Jack was justified by references to chimney sweeps' May Day celebrations in earlier nineteenth-century Guildford, and by references from other Surrey towns that implied that their sweeps were routinely accompanied by Jack in the Green.

John Mason's memories of early Victorian Guildford included the sweeps. 'May Day was the chimney sweeper's holiday. They then dressed in suits after the manner of a harlequin, tinselled and spangled in all the colours of the rainbow, and in groups of five or six performed their peculiar dance, beating out the tune to the music of the shovel and brush and triangle. Town houses and country mansions had to be visited, and in some of the latter they were well entertained, so that their revelry occupied at least a week.'

Not all employers seemed to support the custom. This notice was printed and displayed by one 'J. Loveland, chimney-sweeper, begs to announce that no Boy or Set of Boys in his employ (he having but one little boy in his employ) will parade the streets on the 2nd of May next, J. L. having understood that it is probable that a party or parties are likely to make use of his name, he would ask his friends, as a favor [*sic*], not to bestow on them any money or gift, as no such party have any authority whatever for so using his name. 8, Chapel Street, Guildford April 30, 1853.'

Descriptions of an accompanying Jack occur in several other Surrey towns in the same period. Charles Rose of Dorking recalled (in 1876) that 'May-day was observed much more merrily fifty years ago than now. Then, in addition to that favourite of childhood, the Maypole, and that rarer exhibition on May-day, the garland, there was Jack in the Green surrounded by washed-faced and gaily-decorated sweeps, who, to the sound of hoe and shovel, danced around the whirling Jack in their merriest mood.'

In mid-Victorian Carshalton the sweeps' group had at its centre a Jack in the Green 'in the middle of a hooped erection covered all over with ever-greens and some flowers, with a hole about twelve inches by four inches to see through.'

Benjamin Slater of Mitcham remembered that 'On the first of May the Butchers with marrow Bones and Cleavers, and Chimney-sweeps with a Jack in the Green would go round the village – the sweeps knocked their brushes on their shovels, and the Butchers knocked their marrow bones on their cleavers, there were two flute players as well, which made up the Band. They paid all the nobility of the place a visit, and collected a good sum of money.' (This intriguing reference is the only one I have found from Surrey that records butchers celebrating the day as well as sweeps. It is not clear whether they went round together or as separate groups.)

'The Chimney Sweepers Act of 1864 abolished the employment of boys under 21, though its implementation was patchy. It seems that the Jack did not vanish immediately, however. It may have been maintained for a time by children who were not sweeps, in parallel with their garland-carrying custom. This is one interpretation of the report in 1871 in the *Surrey Advertiser* that, 'May Day was celebrated in Chertsey, the streets being filled with children carrying May poles [i.e. garlands], Jack in the Green, etc.'

Nevertheless, the custom was rapidly declining, possibly as a result of firmer enforcement of employment legislation. J. S. Bright of Dorking wrote in 1884, 'The first of May [has lost] its Jack of the Green, who was clad in leaves and flowers, and seemed to represent the gaiety of the spring by his animation and dance'. The *Croydon Advertiser* in 1887 similarly noted this disappearance. 'The First of May: Though the recurrence of the month of May brings no such general demonstration as used to be associated with it, though Jack in the Green has gone from our midst, and Chimney sweeper's Day is only a memory . . .'

Modern-day Jack in the Greens are often accompanied by musicians and morris dancers, while some engage attendants known as 'bogies', who are attired in green rags adorned with leaves and flowers, and who paint any of their visible flesh green. These go among the crowds daubing onlookers with green face paint, claiming that they are spreading a little of Jack's magic, while children may be presented with small gifts.

Across the country today you will discover revivals, or even completely new Jacks, parading on or around May Day. Some are the focus of their own event, while others are merely participants themselves in a grander affair.

The oldest continual Jack in the Green parades at Knutsford in Cheshire and has done so annually as part of the town's May celebrations every year since 1890, with the exception of the war period.

Knutsford Royal May Day is celebrated on the first Saturday in May. The procession through the town and the crowning of the May Queen, as well as the first appearance of the Jack, was begun in 1864 by the vicar of Knutsford, Revd Robert Clowes, as part of a pageant. The 'Royal' prefix was granted to the event in 1887 by the Prince and Princess of Wales after they had witnessed the May Queen's coronation in person.

The ancient tradition of sanding takes place in the morning, when the route is strewn with coloured sand. Before being associated with May Day, this custom concerned newlyweds, when the path over which they would walk was covered in sand. The practice is said to date back to the reign of King Canute (1018-1035), who once wished a wedding pair 'as many children as there are grains of sand'. In Knutsford today, patterns are often worked into the grains. Jack himself is only one of a number of traditional characters who make an appearance; others include Highwayman Higgins, Robin Hood and Grace Darling.

This grand pageant sets off from Marshall's Yard at 2 p.m. and is then joined by the May Queen and her court at the Sessions House in Toft Road. Hundreds of characters and decorated lorries then make their way along the streets of Knutsford to the Heath, where there is dancing and the crowning ceremony takes place. Spectators can also enjoy displays of maypole dancing and a funfair.

A very interesting point made by Keith Leech in his 2008 book *The Hastings Traditional Jack in the Green*, is that although the Knutsford Jack is of some antiquity, it is not a survivor of an earlier creation but an invented Jack very much in keeping with the Victorian idyll of how they wanted people to perceive old English customs:

> Jacks in the Green were a southern tradition and this is why in northern Knutsford the custom could be prettified. I doubt if the good people of Knutsford had seen the goings on in Hastings and other southern towns and cities in 1864 they would have considered adopting it.

The London suburb of Brentham is the venue for another auspicious May extravaganza which has included a Jack since 1920. This example is promoted as being a walking-talking bush that often perambulates barefoot. The first May Day celebrations at Brentham in the present format were launched on 3 May 1919, central to which were the crowning of the May Queen and dancing around the maypole. The day was a great success, so the following year an improved programme brought Jack in the Green out of retirement, among other things, including the first procession around the neighbourhood. As the years passed, further traditional characters appeared such as Robin Hood and St George, as well as less conventional ones like Tutankhamun, who tapped into the public's imagination at a time when Howard Carter's discovery of the boy king's tomb gripped the land with Egyptian fever.

During the event's subsequent history one particular year is well worth a mention, when Jack and the rest of his compatriots nearly didn't march at all. The year was 1981; up until then there had been an unbroken run, except for the war years, and with just one day to go the organisers of the event were notified by the police of a 28-day ban on any marches in the capital. With incredible speed the May Day organisers arranged a High Court hearing, at which photographs of past processions were presented to the judge. He concluded that the children 'did not look like a very subversive lot' and gave permission for the parade to go ahead.

Brentham May Day is now held on the second Saturday of the month. Jack in the Green parades alongside boys in fancy dress (many togged up as sweeps), Britannia, 150 flower-decked maidens, and of course the resplendent May Queen herself.

Another Jack in the Green appears in Oxford on May Day. It is a revival inaugurated by the Oxford University Morris Men in 1951. Apparently, when they introduced their custom, they believed it to be a new innovation. Later research discovered that during the nineteenth century at least, a Jack had been a common sight in the shadows of the dreaming spires.

One reference to a Jack in the city was uncovered in an edition of the *Oxford University and City Herald* from 3 May 1928, in a story relating to the tragic demise of one of his attendants, described as a 'sweep', who was killed when a horse and carriage ploughed into spectators watching the procession in Blackfriars Road.

On May Day morning the Oxford Jack is first glimpsed near Magdalen Tower just before 6 a.m. Morris sides gather on the city side of Magdalen Bridge to listen to the choir of Magdalen College singing from atop the college tower. After a blessing, Jack leads an informal procession up The High to Radcliffe Square accompanied by musicians, dancers and anyone else who cares to tag along. Here, Jack is at the centre of the first dance of the day, 'Bonny Green', usually around 6.15 a.m.

Further displays of dancing can be enjoyed along the route at places such as New College Lane and Broad Street, before the proceedings conclude with a massed 'Bonny Green Garters' outside St John's College in St Giles at around 8.30 a.m. So, in order to see Oxford's Jack, you will need to be up pretty early.

Following a break for breakfast, most of the morris sides go off to other events around the district. If May Day happens to fall on a weekday, the now merged Oxford University Morris Men and Oxford City Morris Men accompany Jack to St Ebbe's School, where they put on a display for the children.

In 1976 a Jack in the Green was created for the Whitstable Folk Festival and was then revived as part of the town's May Day celebrations. The Jack is now paraded through this Kentish town on May Day, where a procession of dancers and musicians leave the Duke of Cumberland Hotel at 1 p.m. and entertain crowds at the harbour.

The organisation for this event is shared between Herne Bay/Whitstable Lions Club and Oyster Morris, who were themselves formed in 1976 and have both female and male sides. It is interesting to note that the group was started by women and the gents joined later. Oyster Morris includes another character in their ranks called the Green Man, who combines the roles of jester and announcer. His face is painted white on one side and green on the other, and his suit is similarly half white and half festooned with green ribbons.

Also revived in 1976 is the already-mentioned Guildford Bush, who entertains spectators in the Surrey town on the Saturday before the May Day bank holiday, accompanied by the Pilgrim Morris Men. Roger Twitchin, a member of the side, explains:

> The bush is built of Laurel twigs woven into a frame made from green garden netting. Laurel is used as it does not wilt and has fewer insects living in it than a deciduous bush would. Occasionally sprigs of blossom are added to the bush but usually not. The frame contains two shoulder straps and a hole to look out through. The final Jack probably stands about ten inches higher than whoever is carrying it (which has usually been somebody of less than average height).
>
> The activity of the bush depends on the inclination of the carrier. Sometimes it gets in the way of the dancers and entertains the public and at other times it just stands around. For many years the bush was carried by the folklorist George Frampton and it may have been his idea to have a Jack in the Green in Guildford.

One of the most spectacular modern events to include a Jack in the Green is the Rochester Sweeps Festival held over the May Day bank holiday weekend, which began in 1981 to commemorate the one day in the year when sweeps traditionally had a day off and could enjoy themselves away from the soot. In earlier times, the sweeps' holiday was marked by a May Day procession through the streets of Rochester, which included a Jack in the Green. After the passing of the Climbing Boy's Act, the tradition slowly went into decline. The final May celebrations of this ilk were held in the town in the early 1900s.

The modern-day Rochester Sweeps Festival is a three-day fusion of music and dance, with an inevitable Dickensian slant, at which up to a hundred morris sides and other entertainers strut their stuff.

The revived festival is largely attributed to local businessman and ardent amateur historian Gordon Newton, who, having researched the old traditions of the chimney sweeps going back hundreds of years, organised a small parade in 1981 involving a few local morris teams. Under Gordon's guidance, it continued to

Dancers entertain the crowds in front of Rochester Castle during the annual Rochester Sweeps Festival. (© Simon Kelsey)

develop, and is now a major tourist attraction for Kent and has earned millions of pounds for the local economy. Gordon still owns the copyright for the event and maintains the Rochester Sweeps Festival Trust as back-up, should funding ever be withdrawn. Gordon funded the event himself for six years, including all printing and publicity, until it got so large he invited Rochester Council to become involved in its organisation, as well as Doug Hudson, who is now the festival's music producer.

Gordon revived the Rochester Jack in 1983, drawing on accounts recorded by Charles Dickens himself, among others. On May Day morning there is a fascinating ceremony when the Jack is awoken at dawn by dancers and sweeps in the picnic area on nearby Blue Bell Hill, surrounded by twelve bonfires. Again this is based on records of the original custom. On bank holiday Monday he is paraded through the streets, starting in the gardens of Rochester Castle.

In Hastings there is of course the Traditional Jack in the Green Festival, a revival started by Keith Leech in 1983 and which is now one of the biggest annual gatherings of morris dancers in the country. The event is held over the whole of the May Day bank holiday weekend. On the Friday evening you can enjoy folk music sessions in a number of the town's pubs, or a ceilidh in a local hall, while dance sides slowly descend on the borough from around the country. But the festival really gains momentum on the Saturday afternoon, when dancers appear at various spots around the Old Town or along the seafront, areas which have been decorated in advance for the occasion with flowers and ribbons. And in the evening another ceilidh is available for those with reserves of energy.

On Sunday morning a special service for morris dancers is held in one of the Old Town churches, at which a local dancer will perform a solo jig, considered to be a huge honour. The May Queen is crowned in the afternoon and children will put on displays of maypole ribbon plaiting in the grounds of Hastings Castle. All the while further dance performances, folk concerts, and communal dances will continue into the night.

All of this builds up to a spectacular procession on the bank holiday Monday led by the Jack in the Green himself, which starts from the Fishermen's Museum at around 10 a.m. As the Jack reels his way around Hastings Old Town he is immediately followed by local morris sides, including Mad Jack's Morris, chimney sweeps, the May Queen and others from the host community. Then come the visiting morris sides, drummers, and the largest parade of dancing giants currently seen in England.

This procession goes on for much of the morning until it eventually arrives at the Castle around lunchtime, for an afternoon of morris dancing and other

In this picture the Hastings Jack in the Green is accompanied by bogies, themselves dressed in green rags adorned with leaves and flowers. (Courtesy of Colin Bewes)

A scene during the Hastings Traditional Jack in the Green Festival, as Jack is paraded through the streets of Hastings Old Town. (Courtesy of Colin Bewes)

The Hastings Traditional Jack in the Green Festival boasts the largest parade of dancing giants currently seen anywhere in England. (Courtesy of Colin Bewes)

entertainment. The Jack in the Green looks down on the proceedings from on top of the old Norman motte. Eventually, as the event draws to a close, he is led down to the expectant crowd and ceremonially slain in order to release the spirit of summer. His leaves are finally distributed among the crowd and the festival ends for another year.

In the early nineteenth century there were reputed to have been a number of Jack in the Greens evident around Hastings and St Leonards-on-Sea, created by local sweeps such as the Lee family. Their first known mention was in the *Hastings News* of 5 May 1848, in a report that indicated that the custom was well established by that time. Their final tribute was in the *Hastings and St Leonards Chronicle* of 7 May 1884. Keith Leech, who started the current revival based on old newspaper reports and photographs, is a life-long member of Mad Jack's Morris and, during the procession, can still usually be seen disguised as a Bogie. In his book he describes the first year of the current revival, which has since spiralled into the major festival it is today.

At dawn on May 1st 1983 (approximately ninety-nine years after he was last seen), 'Jack in the Green' reappeared on the streets of Hastings. There was no big fanfare it was just a small Jack in the Green with one group of morris dancers out for a good day's dancing. A small photograph heralding the event appeared in the *Hastings Observer*. The Jack in the Green was made from bamboo canes and garden wire held open with hoops, dressed in whatever greenery we could find and fell apart almost as soon as we started to dance with it. It had to be frequently repaired with string and sticky tape. On that first occasion we danced from the Old Town to Silverhill, stopping to dance at the Fire Station and Police Station on the way (as few people were awake at that time in the morning). It was then processed to the St Leonards Gardens for a photograph where the Jack in the Green had been photographed in the nineteenth century.

An extended lunch was then taken at Mr Cherry's public house nearby. Jack in the Green danced along the seafront to the top of the West Hill where it was 'killed' using a theatrical sword, outside the West Hill Café in the early afternoon. It was carried by members of Mad Jack's Morris wearing their usual white morris dance kit. Only one Green Man was represented (by myself), wearing a floral shirt and a pair of green tights! With hindsight it must have been an odd sight indeed!

In Deptford in south-east London, a Jack in the Green was revived in the early 1980s by members of the Blackheath Morris Men and associates, which is known as the Fowlers Troop Jack. Again this is a revival of a Jack who was commonly seen around the area in the early 1900s, which was taken out on May Day by the original Fowlers Troop, the descendants of which now claim the honour. The following is a quote from the *Kentish Mercury* of 18 May 1906:

> It is not more than three or four years since such a band were seen in the streets of Deptford. Jack in his greenery, twirling, and the male and female dancers with him pirouetting something after the traditional style – but there was a sad falling off. In olden days the dancers used to be sweeps, to whom money collected was a sort of annual perquisite and sweeps were very jealous of their privileges in this direction being usurped, latterly however, this rule was by no means adhered to.

All the Jacks we have met so far have been revivals based on original local customs, even though in most cases historical accounts are sketchy to say the least. The City of London Jack in the Green, on the other hand, claims to have no such pedigree and is based on a mixture of illustrations, written descriptions and the influence of other contemporary reincarnations.

In the late 1970s, various morris dancing sides would entertain people in the city by dancing-in the summer when May Day fell during the working week. Leadenhall Market, the Guildhall Yard and several city pubs became the venues for lunchtime performances. Greenwood Morris would dance-in the dawn at Alexandra Palace and then return during the evening, bringing their Jack with them for a tour of London Wall and the Smithfield area.

By 1983, when May Day fell on a Sunday, there were several Jacks going into the smoke. Then, over a lunchtime drink one day, Dave Lobb of the Greenwood Morris Men and Mick Skrzypiec of the Earls of Essex Morris Men, discussed the concept of having an actual City of London Jack in the Green. This led to a brand new creation and its very first outing in 1984, when Mick Skrzypiec, dressed as the Jack, and the Earls of Essex side met at dawn at Wanstead Flats to see in the sunrise. Following breakfast they proceeded by train to Liverpool Street and held the first City of London Jack in the Green procession. With merciless ingratitude, as the ceremony developed over the next few years, the morris element was phased out in order to achieve a more authentic experience.

The City of London Jack in the Green only parades on weekdays, so if May Day falls at the weekend or on the bank holiday, you will probably be out of luck. As well as Jack, the current procession includes musicians, sweeps, bogies and the Lord and Lady of the Ladle. These are aristocratic caricatures, similar I suppose to the eighteenth-century Lord and Lady of the May, who, unlike Jack himself, were so outrageous that thus far nobody has felt the compunction to launch a return of this obnoxious pair.

On the origins of bogies Keith Leech explains:

> The bogies are an interesting phenomenon and entirely modern. I suppose they were the brainchild of Dave Lobb. There is a connection between the London and Hastings Jacks because I am originally a cockney and worked with Dave and Mick on the London Jacks and giants before moving south. Both Dave and Mick come to Hastings as bogies as do some of the Deptford and Carshalton boys. There is a loose fraternity of green men and all are always welcome at the other Jacks. The name appeared in Hastings originally as a childish joke and can be attributed to Brian Chainey.

Keith is also insistent that when discussing the subject of Jack in the Green's, the book by Roy Judge, *The Jack in the Green* (1979) should be mentioned as a contributing source behind many of the current revivals. Keith explains that Roy was from Hastings himself and later moved to London, emphasising, 'it was his book that originally set all of us up doing this'.

In Bristol, a Jack in the Green welcomes the summer each year on the first Saturday in May, in a lively procession through the city's streets accompanied by musicians and dancers. Although there are rumours of Jack's prowling the fair city during the 1860s accompanied by sweeps, the current revival is said to be inspired by the Hastings Festival. The route begins from the historic harbourside outside the Arnolfini, and then visits places like St Nicholas Market, Broadmead, The Horsefair and Redland Grove, before eventually ending the day on Horfield Common, where Jack is slain to release the spirit of summer.

Moving further west again, the town of Ilfracombe in north Devon has paraded a Jack since 2000, which, similar to the one in Bristol, is another descendant of the Hastings Jack. It was introduced to the town's calendar by Lisa Sture and the event takes place on May Day bank holiday Monday. The procession commences at 11 a.m. in Wilder Road car park and winds its way through the High Street and along the seafront towards the harbour area, where children and morris men will dance around the maypole from 12 noon. Jack is finally taken to the beach, where he is stripped of his foliage to release the spirit of summer. His leaves are then distributed on Ilfracombe Pier.

Other Jacks now appear in places like Highworth in Wiltshire, High Wycombe in Buckinghamshire, Winchcombe in Gloucestershire and even Tunbridge Wells in Kent.

Many people today watching the antics of Jack in the Green and his attendant bogies will inevitably see a connection with the mysterious Green Man, whose likeness is sometimes found carved in ancient churches. In pre-Christian England this personification of the spirit of the primeval greenwood was undoubtedly one of the most potent of pagan symbols, regarded as the embodiment of natural fertility. We can gauge his significance by the very fact that his image was adopted by the Christian Church above all other native beliefs, in a bid to seduce the Celts into secular worship.

At the beginning of the chapter, I described Jack's evolution and how historical evidence places his conception to around the eighteenth century, a time when ancient beliefs, you would think, were long forgotten. Romantics among us might not be totally opposed to the idea that these beliefs may have laid dormant in the subconsciousness or even full consciousness of those who first envisaged him, even in very urban settings. However, similar to the Straw Bears discussed earlier, this is extremely unlikely and Jack was probably nothing more than an aid to procure funds.

May Day has long been a defining point of the calendar, announcing as it does the launch of summer in the northern hemisphere. The Celts celebrated May Day as Beltane and it is interesting to conclude with the point that a

Jack in the Green is now an integral player in the Pagan Pride Parade, or Beltane Bash as it is better known, which takes place in Holborn each May. But perhaps most appropriately in the context of this book, he is a perfect illustration of how the customs of our rural ancestors are very much alive and kicking, even in the hustle and bustle of London, one of the largest and most densely populated cities on Earth.

14

RUSHBEARING

RUSHBEARING WAS TRADITIONALLY celebrated in the towns and villages of north-west England. Today, it is still observed in several locations, including Sowerby Bridge in West Yorkshire. The custom derives from the time when the floors of poorer cottages consisted of only the compacted earth on which they were built. Even the floors of basic churches could boast nothing more than bare earth or clay. At one time it was commonplace to bury the bodies of parishioners within the church as well as in the churchyard.

Sweet smelling rushes were used for carpeting people's homes as they had the ability to absorb grease and dirt, and to help purify the air. During the year they were kept fresh by periodically adding new layers and mixing herbs among them. However, at least once a year they would have to be completely cleaned out and replaced. At the same time, members of the community would also attend to the rushes in the church, and eventually this practical act evolved into an annual ceremony, during which the new rushes would be borne to the church on a cart.

Well before the turn of the seventeenth century, this ceremony had become something of a festival in many communities, during which large bundles of rushes were carried to church, often by women. Decorated rushcarts pulled to the church by a company of men started to appear early in the next century. These men would often wear special clothes just for the occasion. It is very uncertain as to when uniform dress became the norm, and, at some places, there may never have been a special uniform dress; this clothing varied at different venues. In 1842, for instance, at the village of Ripponden, an observer described the men as wearing costumes 'something after the manner of

The 1906 Sowerby Bridge rushcart, which was built as part of the town's celebrations to mark the 60th anniversary of local government. (Courtesy of Calderdale MBC)

clown and harlequin in the Christmas pantomime.' At Sowerby Bridge they traditionally wear white shirts, black trousers, Panama hats and clogs. Sixty men would usually pull the cart, with several others following as brakemen.

The rushcart phenomenon spread, but in villages where roads were unsuitable for pulling a cart, the ceremony would be adapted, with the rushes still merely carried to the church in bundles. As the years unfolded the rushcart took on a distinctive form, best-described as a beehive shape. People took huge pride in their decoration. Initially they would be adorned with flowers and garlands, but by the nineteenth century these had been replaced by ever-more elaborate embellishments, such as ribbons, scarves, paper flowers, tinsel, and even personal ornaments and trinkets. A white board or sheet developed at the front of the cart from which silverware might be hung, in the form of pieces of cutlery, trays or mugs, and the whole thing would be surmounted by boughs of oak or ash. The cart had to be of sturdy construction, often supporting loads weighing a ton or more, as well as the fiddler who rode on top to provide music during the procession.

Although rushbearing was not a religious ceremony, the church was, from the beginning, the focal point. In some places it came to coincide with the Wakes holiday. The word 'Wakes' is derived from 'waking' or 'watching', when a vigil would be kept on the eve of a local festival or funeral. As the centuries passed, churches were refurbished with flagstones, so they no longer needed to freshen their floors with rushes, but by this time these festivals had become so popular that their practical function had been superseded by tradition, so their future was secure.

Throughout the nineteenth century rushbearing festivals continued to flourish and it seems that it became increasingly convenient to make them coincide with the old Wakes holiday, which, around Halifax, was now observed in the textile mills as a summer break, taking place in late August or early September. At this time the mills were closed for perhaps a week and the workforce given a holiday while the machinery and other equipment was cleaned and overhauled. At Sowerby Bridge, for instance, this annual holiday was always referred to as the 'Rushbearing', even during years when no cart was crafted.

There is no doubt that rushbearing was a joyous and colourful affair, but there was also a down side. This annual opportunity for working men to let off steam and indulge in a bout of heavy drinking mired the reputation of these glorious events with unruliness, even violence. Peter Thomas, writer and local historian, noted in the 2001 programme for the Sowerby Bridge Rushbearing Festival:

> Our forefathers (and mothers) lived to the full the old maxim of work hard and play hard. Factory hours were long; domestic work without labour-saving appliances was drudgery; life was often cut short by either disease or exhaustion. On the other side of the coin, holidays were brief and rare – but were to be enjoyed to the full! The rushcart procession was still of prime importance, but was only one part of a wider festival of music, dancing, sports, side-shows and, above all, heavy drinking. Community rivalries came to a head as rival rushcarts competed for attention and, stoked up by strong drink, men fell to settling their differences with their fists.

It was this habitual descent into unruliness that effectively brought about the decline of rushbearing towards the end of the nineteenth century. There were two main reasons for this: firstly, because the Church authorities began to distance themselves from the tainted proceedings; and secondly, because many of the mills at the time were owned and run by nonconformists, who deplored strong drink and labelled it 'the working man's curse'. With both the Church and the establishment increasingly abhorred by the disorderly outcome of such festivals, they became less important and were reduced to little more than a small sideshow within a larger funfair. In many places they faded away altogether.

However, rushbearing had become so rooted in popular culture that revivals were inevitable. By the early part of the twentieth century, it was set to enjoy just such a revival at Sowerby Bridge, when, in 1906, a rushcart was built. In that particular year, celebrations planned to mark the 60th anniversary of local government presented an opportunity to build one. Although these had been absent from the town for all of that time, they simmered in the popular psyche.

A huge crowd turned out to witness the spectacle of the cart being hauled along the town's main street by thirty robust men, who, for the main part, were local canal bargees (the Rochdale Canal passes through the town). The wooden front was decked with flowers and a fiddler sat astride the top behind a curious triangular shape, while the procession was complimented by the presence of the Horwich Morris Men. To this day the origin of the said triangular shape on Sowerby's cart causes disagreement among local people. Some say it represents a symbolic tree, others that it shows the Holy Trinity, or the three parishes included in the celebrations. But more likely the origin of this triangle is in the decorated garlands seen at other rushbearings. They were similar in shape and often carried on top of the cart.

In spite of the popularity of the 1906 event, it was only ever intended to be a one-off and no further rushcarts would grace the streets of Sowerby Bridge for the next seventy-one years. But in 1977 it was planned to include one in celebrations marking the Silver Jubilee of Queen Elizabeth II. This second revival and indeed the building of the rushcart itself was very much due to the efforts of two people, Fred Knights and Garry Stringfellow. Fred, who is life president of the Rushbearing Committee, married a girl from Sowerby Bridge and afterwards settled in the town, working first as a policeman, then as an educational officer and finally as a social worker. Local man Garry on the other hand was a tool maker, the proprietor of the town's fish and chip shop, and school teacher for twenty-five years.

As plans for the Jubilee progressed, the decision was taken to hold the rushbearing in September, its traditional time, and not to include it within the Jubilee celebrations in July. In separating these two events, the rushbearing gained a

The revival at Sowerby Bridge began in 1977, when a rushcart was built as part of the Queen's Silver Jubilee celebrations. The festival has taken place annually, from that day to this. (Courtesy of Calderdale MBC)

momentum all of its own that would thereafter firmly establish it as an important annual fixture in the Sowerby Bridge calendar.

The 1977 Sowerby Bridge Rushbearing was a half-day event that took place in the afternoon of Saturday 3 September. Rushes were distributed between four separate churches, Christ Church and Tuel Lane Methodist in Sowerby Bridge itself, and St George's and St Peter's in the village of Sowerby. The procession included the Horwich Morris Men, the Kirkburton Rapier Dancers, choirs from all four participating churches, and the Tuel Lane Methodist Church Scout and Guide Band. A new and welcome innovation was the replacement of the fiddler with a cart maiden. This might have seemed a glamorous role but it was a bumpy and precarious ride over cobbled streets, and none of the men were prepared to do it. The maiden was tasked with lowering the triangle to avoid branches or other obstacles.

Rushbearing has taken place at Sowerby Bridge each year since 1977 and, during that time, has evolved into a two-day festival occurring on the first weekend in September. From 1978 onwards it became the custom for the rush-cart to stop at each public house along its 10-mile route, in order for the sixty pullers and ten brakemen to enjoy liquid refreshment. At every stop, whether it is a church, pub, or market place, sides of morris dancers from both near and far would entertain the crowd. These would include women's morris sides and clog-dancing teams. The Bradshaw Mummers annually perform their very own brand of ritual drama, and in more recent times a whole team of cart maid-ens will take it in turn to ride atop the swaying cart.

The modern-day cart takes around ten days to prepare under the direction of the cart manager. It is decorated with tightly fastened bundles of rushes, tradi-tionally cut at Fly Flatts near Warley Moor in late August. Every effort is made to improve on the previous year and it is with some sadness that the rushcart is stripped and mothballed at the close of festivities. Mind you, at the end of the 1991 festival the cart was almost totally lost, when some local youngsters thought it would be fun to set it alight as it rested behind St Bartholomew's Church in Ripponden. Luckily, one of the pullers lived close by and did much to save it before the arrival of the fire brigade. The following year the refur-bished cart was called the 'Phoenix Cart'.

The current event kicks-off on the Friday evening, with pubs in the area putting on barbecues and live music. There is also a pre-festival get-together for all the organisers, cart pullers and morris dancers. The weekend festivities also include a traditional fair held in the canal basin, with street entertainers, special church services, a market, the Real Ale Trail in Sowerby Bridge, a fête and flower festival in Ripponden, and many other attractions. But the rushbearing processions on Saturday and Sunday remain the most important elements of this summer gala.

The present Saturday route begins at St John's Church, Warley, at 10.15 a.m. It then presents rushes at St Patrick's, Christ Church, and St Paul's, all in Sowerby Bridge, before ending at Hollins Mill Lane around 17.10 p.m. On Sunday, the procession commences from St Peter's Church, Sowerby village, at 12 noon , and continues to St Mary's at Cottonstones, and St Bartholomew's at Ripponden, concluding at around 4.45 p.m. Along both routes several hos-telries are visited, including those with the evocative names The Maypole Inn and The Rushcart Inn.

The front of the rushcart, which is pulled during Littleborough's Rushbearing Festival. (Courtesy of Rochdale Online)

Social rather than excessive drinking is today associated with the festival, which, in its modern form, fails to attract the unruliness of earlier times and enjoys the whole-hearted blessing of the Church. In fact, it has become something of a tradition following the morning service at St Peter's, Sowerby, for the vicar of that parish to ride on top of the rushcart from the church to its first port of call, the Rushcart Inn. Peter Thomas wrote that 'according to good authority, the experience always puts the vicar in need of at least one stiff brandy!'

Rushcarts are still also regularly paraded at two other spots in the south Pennines, Littleborough near Rochdale, and in the Saddleworth Valley. The current revival at Littleborough dates back to 1991 and was instigated by Rochdale Morris and the Littleborough Action Group. It is a two-day festival in July, where, on the Saturday, a rushcart proceeds from the King William IV public house to St Barnabas' Church, where rushes are blessed. After the church service morris dancing takes place at the Caldermoor Inn and Littleborough town square, before the procession ends at Harehill Park for a range of activities. On Sunday morning, the festivities continue with the rushcart leaving Rakewood Rugby Club and ending at the town square again, with various stops along the way for the crowd to enjoy further morris dancing from both local and visiting groups, as well as music from various bands.

In the Saddleworth Valley, the tradition was revived in 1975 largely due to the efforts of Peter Ashworth and the Saddleworth Morris Men. Once again, the tradition here had died out in the early twentieth century. Apparently the rushcart of 1889 was so poorly built that it fell to pieces!

Today, the rushes for the cart are collected from the surrounding moors. Saddleworth Moor is of course on the edge of the Peak District National Park, and permission to gather the rushes is granted by the National Trust. The two-day festival takes place on the second weekend following the 12 August, and on the Saturday the rushcart, known as 'The Saddleworth Longwood Thump Rushcart', is pulled through the various villages of the valley by 150 men. A member of the Saddleworth Morris Men sits astride the rushcart for the day, provided with ale from a copper kettle. On Sunday, the rushcart is taken to St Chad's Church, Uppermill, where the top is dismantled and the rushes are mixed with herbs and flowers before being symbolically spread in the aisles. After the service there is an afternoon's entertainment with displays of English male traditional dance, musicianship, gurning, clog-stepping, a competition to find the worst singer, and, weather permitting, a wrestling competition contested by morris men only.

Rushbearing is also celebrated at five places in Cumbria, but without a rush-cart. Central to the processions at these is a cross made from rushes or flowers, while people of all ages carry elaborate shapes called 'rushbearings', some as large as 4 or 5ft tall. Traditional shapes for the rushbearings include harps, crosses, and maypoles. These processions are usually led by a band, followed by representatives of the clergy, the villagers carrying the rushbearings, and the children of the village. They end at the local church with hymns and prayers.

These ceremonies are held on, or near to the saint's days of the churches in question. At St Mary's Church in Ambleside, this will be the first Saturday in July; at St Columba's Church at Warcop, 29 June (unless Sunday, then 28 June); St Theobold's Church at Great Musgrave, first Saturday in July; and St Mary and St Michael's Church in Urswick on the Sunday nearest St Michael's Day, which is on 29 September. St Oswald's Church in Grasmere is slightly different. Originally it was held on 20 July, being the old celebration of St Peter, but was changed to 5 August, St Oswald's Day, from 1885 onwards. In 2003, the date was again changed back to July to coincide with the last Saturday of Grasmere School's summer term, in order to include all the children in the celebration.

Each of these festivals is slightly different. At Grasmere, for instance, token rushes are carried on a special linen sheet, held by six girls dressed in green and who are known as the Rush Maidens. Traditionally, the children of Grasmere and Ambleside are given a piece of Grasmere gingerbread if they have carried

At Grasmere, these children parade a rushbearing in the traditional form of a maypole. (Courtesy of Ann Bowker)

one of the rushes. Some of the festivals are accompanied by children's sports, including Ambleside which are organised by the fire brigade, the highlight of which is the children's Fell race to Todd Crag and back. And at both Warcop and Great Musgrave, children wear elaborately decorated crowns.

The true purpose of rushbearing in any of its forms is hard to understand, celebrating as it does a domestic labour of centuries past. It might have a connection to the Christian Church, but it definitely has the feel of a more ancient pagan ritual. There is no evidence to support it having any pagan origins, but as its beginnings were in pre-Puritan times, the Puritan Church tried to suppress the ceremonial side of the event as they saw it as another Popish activity. No doubt rushes were used for carpeting in Celtic huts long before Christianity entered these shores. Even Peter Thomas, who has studied its history and tradition, begged the question: 'When all is said and done – when the procession has passed, and the beer has been drunk and the merriment is over – a question remains. What on earth is it all about?'

15

WELL DRESSING

L IKE MANY RURAL customs, the origins of well dressing are lost in antiquity and although it has been practised in many counties, it has become particularly associated with Derbyshire, where some water sources were thought to have healing qualities, so the wells were decorated in Druid rituals as a way of giving thanks to the water gods. The early Christian Church tried to ban the custom along with all other forms of water worship, but similar to rushbearing, it refused to be forgotten and was adapted to become acceptable to the Church. One way of doing this was by dedicating wells to Christian saints, an early example being St Ann's well in Buxton.

Well dressing is the art of decorating wells with pictures made from the petals of flowers and other natural components, such as moss, nuts, leaves, seeds or bark. These brightly coloured collages are normally of a religious nature, or might illustrate myths and legends, historical figures, or a local custom. Variations of this art have been practised all around the UK. For instance, in Scotland and Cornwall pieces of coloured rags are tied to the boughs of trees which overhang water sources. These are known as Cloutie wells in the North and Clootie wells in the South, and probably even pre-date the Derbyshire dressings. Similar dressings are also known in both Ireland and Wales, so it is evident that they are of Celtic origin, the obvious link between all these regions. Here the people of ancient Britain continued to thrive long after a succession of invasions of these Isles, and where their descendants still proudly survive today, holding on to some of their ancient traditions. But in Derbyshire, the local people evolved a distinctive style all of their own. The pictures are set in a layer of wet clay that is spread over a framed backing board to a depth of about two inches. Into this clay, thousands of petals are meticulously pressed by hand. The clay has to be kept moist or it will crack and the petals will fall away. When the picture is finished, the board is mounted on a wooden frame and erected at the site of a well.

Of course, the dressings were not always quite so elaborate. In pagan times the wells would have been adorned with nothing more than seasonal foliage and flowers, progressing to garlands in the fullness of time. But around 200 years ago, floral cameos were introduced for the first time, initially illustrating water subjects, such as rivers or waterfalls. These eventually made way for biblical scenes, again depicting stories of an aquatic nature: Noah's ark, Jonah and the whale, or the parting of the Red Sea, being obvious choices.

Today, these dressings can be extremely time-consuming to make and villagers will often work right through the night prior to the start of a festival, to make certain the plants they use are as fresh as possible. Some people have been known to craft their dressings in secret, in order to unveil them in their full glory on the first morning of the event. Once erected, the dressing will usually

'Jonathan warns David': a well dressing at Tissington in 2008 that draws on a biblical theme. (Courtesy of Sir Richard FitzHerbert)

This picture, taken in front of North Mill in Belper, shows traditional well dressing panels made by local primary school children for the town's annual Well Dressing Festival in 2005. (Courtesy of Ann Pocklington)

last about a week before the petals begin to lose their lustre and start to fade. In hot weather there is a danger that the clay will quickly crack, while in blustery conditions, the product of so much hard work does not remain pristine for long.

This custom is still mainly observed in the limestone towns and villages of the Peak District, where the season stretches from May to September. Of the more significant venues, Tissington is traditionally first in late May, while Eyam is the last in late August.

Shortly after a dressing has been erected, members of the clergy and community gather at the site for a short blessing service while a brass band provides suitable music. The description 'well' is used loosely, as sometimes the water source is a pump, tap, or trough. Some people have even been known to dress places where no well of any description exists. These can hardly be classed as well dressings, although it seems the people who erect them certainly consider them as such. But whatever they are, most towns or villages have several examples, so a procession ensues in order to visit and bless each one in turn. In some places, this well blessing ceremony is the official starting point for a week-long celebration or 'wake', culminating with a carnival.

Perhaps the oldest known site to have enjoyed centuries of this style of well dressing is Tissington, a pretty village near Ashbourne. For centuries this has been a typical estate village, where the inhabitants have worked for the lords of the manor. Tissington Hall is the ancestral home of the FitzHerbert family, today represented by Sir Richard FitzHerbert. The tradition here can be traced back to just after the Black Death of 1348-49. Although elsewhere the population was ravaged by plague, Tissington escaped the horrors and its immunity was ascribed to the purity of the water, so it became customary to decorate the wells in thanksgiving.

Later, in 1615, there was a long, dry, summer and severe drought, when crops failed and thousands of cattle perished. Between the end of March and early August, it is said that rain fell on only three occasions. But despite the severity of the drought, Tissington's five wells continued to flow and the surrounding district had cause to be grateful for the unending supply of water coming from this little village.

To celebrate their deliverance, the people again dressed the wells and held a thanksgiving service. Apparently, this custom, held on Ascension Day, has continued ever since with relatively few breaks, such as during the two world wars and the 2001 outbreak of Foot and Mouth disease. The five wells here, called Hall Well, Town Well, Coffin Well, Hand's Well and Yew Tree Well, are all at the sites of genuine springs, which means that if the villagers ever experience problems with their piped water supply, they will still be served by this unending and fresh reserve.

But why was well dressing so widely practised in Derbyshire? Did the people living there somehow know and appreciate the fact that their water was of a much better quality than that of other areas? The town of Buxton is particularly noted for having some of the purest water in the world, and, reputedly, the only true thermal water in Derbyshire. Emerging from nine springs in the Crescent area of the town, this faintly blue-coloured water is the reason why Buxton grew as a spa resort. The Romans knew it as 'Aqua Arnemetiae' meaning 'The Spa of the Goddess of the Grove'. This name was unquestionably borrowed from the Celts, who venerated wells and believed that goblins, fairies or elves watched over them. One of the most famous was known as 'Artemis'. Another Celtic water sprite was called Santan. So, did the local people here cleverly disguise their pagan beliefs when they named St Ann's Well to please the clergy?

The bottled water we can buy today is said to have fallen as rain some 5,000 years ago. It then undertakes an epic journey through subterranean depths, during which it interacts with heat-giving minerals, warming it to around 27.5° Centigrade. If this is all true, and the waters of the Peak District do percolate so timelessly, we can perhaps begin to understand how, in 1615, the waters of Tissington continued to flow with utter disregard for the pervading drought.

At Buxton, St Ann's Well became noted as a place of pilgrimage for hundreds of people suffering from a variety of illnesses. By this time, it was more likely that these pilgrims believed fervently in the healing powers of the saint, rather than the possibility that the water itself contained curative properties. Perhaps the most celebrated visitor was the rheumatic Mary Queen of Scots, who visited the waters at least four times during her exile in the area. These pilgrims would leave votive offerings to illustrate their faith, such as crutches, or even effigies of their inflicted body parts. This became so well known that Thomas Cromwell, Henry VIII's notorious chancellor, ordered the destruction of all well-worshiping paraphernalia, which the new religious order regarded as un-Christian, even blasphemous.

There are three principle wells in Buxton that are now regularly dressed: St Ann's Well, Taylor's Drinking Well, and the Higher Buxton Well. The first recorded dressing took place in 1840, after the Duke of Devonshire arranged to have a supply of water piped from Cold Springs on the edge of the town to the Market Place. In gratitude the town's folk dressed the pump, and a subsequent well has been decorated on the same site ever since. A procession has always been another aspect of the occasion right from that very first dressing in 1840, which in its descendant form is now a spectacular carnival.

Well dressing continued in Buxton throughout the remainder of the nineteenth century, until a final event was held in 1912, when Miss Ida Berry was crowned the Festival Queen. Many of the pre-war dressings were the work of local man William Brunt. However, recognising its value as a tourist attraction, the town council reintroduced it in 1925, when Miss Florence Morten was crowned Festival Queen. This was also the first year that the Church was fully involved and a team of people were employed by the council to administer to the boards. In 1947, a Well Dressing Committee was appointed, by which time the occasion had spiralled into a major festival for the town. Since 1986, when the local council withdrew its financial support, the dressings have been made by volunteers, who collectively repair the boards, puddle the clay, draw the new designs, and then dress and erect the annual offerings. Around fifty people invest countless hours to uphold the town's tradition, and much of the work is carried out at St John the Baptist's Church, where visitors are welcome to see the various processes being undertaken.

Chris Simpson, the secretary of the Buxton Wells Dressing Festival, explains that those interested in the history of the event may notice from old photographs that the boards vary in shape. This is because the boards used immediately after 1925 were from Wirksworth, and those responsible for them were paid by the council to dress the wells in Buxton. This situation continued until the council

Well dressing at the old pump in the Market Place in Chesterfield in 2002, celebrating the Queen's Golden Jubilee. (Photo courtesy of Glyn Williams)

workmen eventually made some new boards of their own. These were then used right up until the millennium, when the Festival Committee had new boards made.

The blessing of the wells now takes place on the Sunday before the second Wednesday in July, with the carnival on the Saturday after the second Wednesday. As well as the dressing in the Market Place, which is now the location of a funfair during the latter part of the festival week, there are dressings at St Ann's Well in The Crescent, and a drinking fountain dressed by children in Spring Gardens, which is known as Taylors Drinking Fountain.

The festival now encompasses a wide range of events, of which the Saturday carnival is the pinnacle. But carnival day involves much more than just a procession. It includes the judging of decorated vehicles, tableaux, and foot characters, the duck race, and the 5-mile carnival day road race. The carnival procession itself begins at 2 p.m. when the Wells Dressing Festival Queen, Rosebud and retinue, take up position on the festival coach at the head of the pageant. Afterwards, visiting Queens, Rosebuds and their retinues from other towns and villages are received by the Buxton Wells Dressing Festival Queen and invited to compete in the Parade of Queens in the Pavilion Gardens.

But if Tissington heralds the start of the well dressing season and Buxton is among its high points, Eyam brings it to a close. Eyam village is famed in history for completely quarantining itself in 1665, when it suffered from a strain of bubonic plague. Nobody was allowed in or out, and although the actions of the villagers did indeed prevent the disease from spreading to the wider world, it was at the cost of virtually the entire population. The current revival here began at the time of the Festival of Britain in 1951. In point of fact, there are no true wells in the village, which instead boasts one of the earliest piped water supplies in the country, installed in 1588 to feed a series of water troughs. To celebrate the Festival of Britain, it was some of these very troughs that were dressed for the occasion. Nowadays three symbolic water troughs are dressed: these are the Townhead Well at the western end of the village, and the Town End Well and Children's Well, which stand close together near the village square.

Eyam Carnival and Wakes Week occurs towards the end of August. It begins on the Saturday prior to the last Sunday in August, which is known as Plague Sunday, and in line with the traditional pattern, it kicks off with the blessing of the wells. On carnival day the main parade, with floats and local queens, commences from the village square at 3 p.m. During the intervening days activities might include a clay pigeon shoot, beetle drive, fell race and sheep roast.

On Plague Sunday itself, a religious service is also held at Eyam to remember those who perished in the plague. This is held at Cucklet Delph, a nearby valley where outdoor worship apparently took place during those cursed days, rather than in the closer confines of the parish church. A procession now makes its way from Eyam church to Cucklet Delph, where a special hymn is sung.

Today, although Derbyshire can still claim to be the historical homeland of well dressing, it no longer has a monopoly on this attractive art form, which spread into neighbouring counties many years ago. For instance, it was reintroduced into east Cheshire in 2001 at Sutton, near Macclesfield, where it is still going strong. Much Wenlock in Shropshire has been dressing since 1996; Endon in Staffordshire has one of the longest traditions anywhere, and Penistone is among those to champion the cause in South Yorkshire.

But well dressing has reached communities even farther afield, such as Frome in Somerset, which has been dressing since 1989, while Upwey, near Weymouth in Dorset, has been dressing since 2002. This is an appropriate site for a well dressing, as it is believed that Weymouth was the port through which the plague first entered Britain, an event that proved the catalyst for much of the well-dressing tradition. Corfe Castle in Dorset included a well dressing as part of a flower festival at the Church of St Edward King & Martyr in 2008. Caistor in Lincolnshire erected four well dressings in July 2000 as part of their Millennium celebrations. These featured a Roman centurion, England's largest sheep, a broken cross and risen Christ, and the devastating fire of Caistor, all subjects relevant to the history of the town.

Bisley, near Stroud in Gloucestershire, is often claimed to be an example of a well dressing site, but, although it does have a long-standing tradition of decorating its well with floral motifs for Ascension Day, its dressing does not have the defining characteristics of the Derbyshire style, namely the picture or design made of natural materials pressed onto a board. The custom was established by the Revd Thomas Keble in 1863, after he had tidied up and formalised the village's main water supply in Wells Road. Today, a short church service is followed by a procession to the wells where wreaths and posies are laid. The eldest twenty-two children in the Bluecoat village school carry the wreaths and garlands that head the procession and form the centrepiece of the ceremony. These consist of Stars of David, the letters AD and the year, letters spelling out 'Ascension Day' and five hoops.

Well dressing, or 'well flowering' as it was once known, is a particularly beautiful custom and another in which people in the community take enormous pride. It is also a custom which, in many villages, caters for children, who often make their own dressings, thus ensuring its survival for future generations: for they are the petallers in waiting. The fun of the experience for many children is the gathering of the flowers themselves, which can be obtained from gardens

This well dressing in the Market Place in Derby in 2008 depicts the Ram of local fame. (Photo courtesy of Glyn Williams)

or in the countryside, although it has to be pointed out that most English wild flowers are now protected by law.

In earlier days the availability of materials used for well dressing was very much governed by the natural flora that was blooming at the time of the event. As the well-dressing season stretches over several months and each town or village dressed their wells at different times, it meant the catalogue of flowers, seeds and mosses employed was incredibly diverse. Inevitably some flowers were grown with well dressing specifically in mind, while, later, it was not uncommon for flowers to be imported from abroad and coloured with natural dyes. Among the well-dressing fraternity today the Hydrangea family is a firm favourite as their petals bloom over a relatively long season. They can also be nurtured in lovely deep shades of pink, blue or white, depending on the acidity of the soil in which they are grown. A variety called Mme E. Moullere does particularly well in Derbyshire as it relishes the limey soil. Other modern favourites include Eucalyptus, Chrysanthemums, Carnations, and the commercially grown Gerbera, all of which have strong petals compared to some other varieties of flower.

The following is an alphabetical list of other places that have celebrated well dressing in recent years, although the list is almost certainly not comprehensive. (Derbyshire): Aldercar, Ashford-in-the-Water, Aston-upon-Trent, Ault Hucknall, Bakewell, Bamford, Barlborough, Barlow, Baslow, Belper, Bolehill, Bolsover, Bonsall, Brackenfield, Bradwell, Brimington, Buxworth, Chapel-en-le-Frith, Charlesworth, Chatsworth, Chelmorton, Chesterfield, Clay Cross, Clowne, Coal Aston, Cressbrook, Cromford, Cutthorpe, Dale Abbey, Derby, Dronfield, Dronfield Woodhouse, Earl Sterndale, Elmton, Elton, Etwall, Foolow, Glapwell, Glossop, Great Hucklow, Great Longstone, Hackney, Hadfield, Hartington, Hathersage, Hayfield, Heage, Heath, Holmesfield, Holmewood, Holymoorside, Hope, Horsley Woodhouse, Killamarsh, Kniveton, Little Longstone, Litton, Marston Montgomery, Matlock, Middleton, Milford, Millthorpe, Monyash, Norbury, Ockbrook, Old Tupton, Old Whittington, Osmaston, Over Haddon, Palterton, Peak Forest, Pilsley, Pleasley, Riber, Ridgeway, Ripley, Rowsley, Rowthorne, Shirebrook, Spondon, Starkholmes, Stoney Middleton, Swanwick, Taddington, Tansley, Tibshelf, Tideswell, Tintwhistle, Unstone, Upper Langwith, Waingroves, Wardlow, Wessington, West Hallam, Whaley Bridge, Whitwell, Wingerworth, Wirksworth, Wormhill, Wyaston, and Youlgreave. (Staffordshire): Brewood, Brown Edge, Burton-upon-Trent, Flash, Grindon, Hollinsclough, Ipstones, Kingstone, Lichfield, Longnor, Marchington, Middle Mayfield, Newborough, Upper Tean, and Werrington. (South Yorkshire): Conisborough, Dore, Harthill, Norton, Ravenfield, Wath-upon-Dearne, and Wickersley. (Cheshire): Beeston, Bollington, and Mickle Trafford. (Greater Manchester): Chadkirk, Compstall, and Gee Cross. (Nottinghamshire): Headon, and Scarcliffe.

16

FIRE FESTIVALS

O NE OF HUMANKIND'S fundamental achievements is the ability to harness the element of fire. They could create flames to warm their homes and cook their food; it could be employed as a weapon of war; and its properties were used to industrialise emerging civilisations. Ancient man would have both feared and revered fire with equal respect. Fire gods would have ranked among their most important deities. The Celts, for instance, had Taranis the god of thunder and lightning. It is difficult for us today to truly appreciate the need for these gods, but possibly Taranis was perceived as the sky-god who could unleash great powers from the heavens, which were thought to indicate anger directed against human activities on earth. Among these powers, fire was the most potent. Such gods, including the mighty Thor, were often seen as blacksmiths generating destruction from their celestial forges. It was inevitable, therefore, that fire festivals would hold a place in ancient society and that today their embers would still flicker in various traditions around the country.

Every year in Cornish towns and villages people observed fire festivals, which in their original pre-Christian format were midsummer celebrations at one time popular throughout the country, but particularly so in the Penwith area around Penzance and Newlyn. These celebrations would have varied from place to place, but would certainly have included the lighting of great bonfires and processions of young men carrying burning torches and barrels between the villages. In time, these celebrations came to coincide with the period between St John's Eve, held on 23, June and St Peter's Eve, on 28 June. In Penzance they were called the Golowan Festival, and, in the ancient Cornish tongue, Golowan or Goluan meant the feast of St John.

During the nineteenth century Penzance had become the focus for these widespread bonfire and firework festivities, when every year, on 23 June, the streets of the town were said to be choked by thick, acrid smoke. Towards the end of the night, local youths would jump over or pass themselves through the smouldering embers of the flames. No doubt St John's Eve was also marked with the consumption of copious quantities of alcohol, making these youths ever more daring and susceptible.

In 1754, Dr William Borlase described these celebrations in his book *Antiquities of Cornwall*. He noted how the Cornish attended their fires with 'lighted torches, tarr'd and pitch'd at the end' and with them processed from village to village. He further added:

> This is certainly the remains of the Druid superstition, for 'faces praeferre', to carry lighted torches, was reckoned a kind of Gentilism, and as such particularly prohibited by the Gallick Councils: they were in the eye of the law 'accensores facularum', and thought to sacrifice to the devil, and to deserve capital punishment.

Penzance Borough Council was determined to bring an end to these celebrations and, using the argument that they were a fire risk to the town with implications on insurance premiums, in the 1890s they finally succeeded in having them banned. And so they might have remained, had it not been for the attentions of the Old Cornwall Society, who, in the 1920s, adopted Golowan as the basis for their midsummer bonfire celebrations.

In 1990, Penzance Town Council, several local schools, and a small group of artists and historians got together to revive the festival, with health and safety always at the forefront of their considerations. Since then it has grown to become a major arts and culture event that brings tens of thousands of people to the town each year. The showpiece of the modern festival is known as Mazey Day, but there are still many aspects of the old one incorporated, including fireworks.

The Golowan Festival is now a colourful cocktail of ingredients both ancient and new, which normally runs for nine days in late June, with the finale weekend being the one nearest to St John's Eve. Among these ingredients is Penglaz, the Penzance 'Obby 'Oss. Like other hobby horses he is no doubt of ancient origin, although he is first described in the nineteenth century as an integral part of the entertainment staged by mummers and guisers. The modern Penglaz makes his appearance late at night beguiling and frightening the Golowan revellers. The creature is based on descriptions of Penglaz found in old texts, and is sur-

The Mazey Day parade in Penzance during the Golowan Festival. (Courtesy of Simon Reed)

rounded by secrecy and myth. Also taking to the streets are the Golowan Band, an ad hoc group of musicians who traditionally played during the fiery carnival.

The day that followed the hedonic excesses associated with the fire festival was altogether more sedate and civilised, and included the Quay Fair, when people could walk around market stalls, take boat trips around the harbour, and eat strawberries. By evening there would be music and merriment, and once again a lot of drinking, which in Penzance was permitted due to an ancient charter that allowed all the public houses near the Quay to stay open for twenty-four hours. Today, the Quay Fair is still a lively part of the revived festival.

The serpent dance is another old Penzance custom performed through the streets of the town. Men and women, young and old, would all join hands to form a giant coiling serpent, and with the cry of 'an eye, an eye', it would rush through an arch of hands in its own length. The dance was traditionally executed on St John's Eve. In Celtic tradition the snake or serpent symbolises regeneration and in most ancient societies it was seen as a good omen, illustrated by its representation on the staff of Mercury and its use as a universal symbol of medicine. Another part of the festival is the crowd's election of a mock mayor, whose tenure lasts until the end of the celebrations.

The serpent dance is performed at the Golowan Festival fire celebration in Penzance. (Courtesy of Simon Reed)

The core of today's festival is the three days of the weekend around St John's Eve. These are known as Mazey Eve on Friday, Mazey Day on Saturday and Quay Fair Day on Sunday. Mazey Eve includes the Summer Fire, which is a spectacular fireworks display that takes place at the end of an evening of light-hearted fun around the Jubilee Pool on the Promenade. Saturday is a large community and arts celebration. The streets are closed as artists, school-children and even members of the public take part in a series of processions that include music, giant sculptures, and a variety of other artistic genres. The Golowan band leads the Mazey Day processions and will also be found playing throughout the festival in many unlikely locations around the town. Musicians and artists from other Celtic nations are also now a regular feature, as are a variety of other musical contributors. Performances take place at several venues, including the Acorn Theatre and the Golowan Marquee, which is erected adjacent to St Anthony's Gardens. Penzance itself is decorated with large amounts of banners and greenery, echoing the practice in the town during the ancient festival. Mazey Day attracts thousands of visitors to the area and has become an important symbol of the town's identity. The Quay Fair on Sunday is a celebration of the harbour's maritime links, with visiting boats welcomed and decorated to add to the festive atmosphere. The day is also a throwback to the midsummer fairs of old, with market stalls, rides, and street entertainment.

One place which still upholds the ancient tradition of lighting a midsummer bonfire is the village of Whalton in Northumberland, which is 6 miles west of Morpeth. In a history of Durham and Northumberland printed in 1828, it was described as 'one of the neatest and cleanest villages in the county'.

The annual ceremony held here, which takes place on the village green just outside the local pub, the Beresford Arms, is known as the Whalton Bale, which takes place every midsummer's eve, or 4 July. Whalton is believed to be the only village in England to have perpetuated this once commonplace observance since 1903. It is claimed to be a relic of the series of great bonfires that the ancient Britons lit throughout the year to mark the progress of the sun. Other Northumberland villages have been known to organise an annual bale since that time, but these are held in the winter, not on midsummer's eve.

The actual word 'bale' originated in Northumberland and comes from a time when rural parts of the county were under constant threat from the attack of Reivers. These were gangs of men who would raid along both sides of the Anglo-Scottish border from the late thirteenth century to the beginning of the seventeenth century, usually to steal cattle of horses. These cut-throat bands consisted of both Scottish and English families, raiding the entire border area without regard to the nationality of their victims. The local farmers developed fortified homes into which their livestock could be shepherded if Reivers were known to be in the vicinity. Beacon fires would be lit on hilltops or high places to warn of approaching danger, and these they called 'bales'. Having said that, there is some disagreement about the spelling of the word, with some people insisting that it should be 'baal', from the Anglo-Saxon word for fire, derived from the name of the sun-god Bel, or Baal.

As well as sporting a fine bonfire, the Whalton Bale is now a festival at which sides of morris dancers entertain the crowd. There might also be sword dancers, fiddlers and pipers. Groups of children hold hands to dance around the fire. At one time, similar to the fires in Cornwall, young people would leap through the flames, a tradition since abandoned for obvious reasons. After the outside entertainment is over and the fire has burnt its course, the revelers retire to the village hall for refreshments and to enjoy a barn dance. Whalton is still 'one of the neatest and cleanest villages in the county', which in 2002 had the distinction of winning the Best Kept Small Village Award.

Another fire-related custom practised on the last Thursday in October in a number of villages in Somerset is Punkie Night, which bears striking similarities to the way in which Halloween is celebrated in the United States of America and latterly here in England as well.

The most popular place to observe this ritual is the village of Hinton St George near Crewkerne where children parade around the streets carrying Jack o' lanterns called 'Punkies' and singing the Punkie Night song, which goes:

It's Punkie Night tonight
It's Punkie Night tonight
Adam and Eve would not believe
It's Punkie Night tonight

It's Punkie Night tonight
It's Punkie Night tonight
Give us a candle give us a light
It's Punkie Night tonight

Traditional Jack o' lanterns as sported on Halloween, are of course made from pumpkins, whereas the Punkie version is carved from a mangel-wurzel, or possibly even a swede. The word 'Punkie' is thought to be an Old English term for a lantern, although another theory is that it derives from the word 'spunky' by which people on the Somerset Levels referred to balls of light that rise up from the marshes, which are also known as 'Will-o-the-wisps'. These were believed to be the souls of children who died before christening and thus doomed to wander the moors until Judgement Day, although they are in effect pockets of escaping bog gas, or methane.

The story behind the festival has little to do with courting the dead as in Halloween, but is said to originate probably from the nineteenth century when men from the village would get drunk and tarry at a fair held annually at nearby Chiselborough. To help them navigate home in the dark their wives would fashion lanterns by hollowing out a mangel-wurzel, putting a candle inside it, and attaching it to several pieces of cord so that it could be carried puppet style.

Another version of this saga claims that the very first time this happened was because, on one particular night the ladies of the village had grown so concerned about the late return of their spouses from the fair, that they went in search of them, carrying Punkies to light their way. The drunken husbands saw the eerie lights approaching and thought they were goolies, and fled in terror. This round-up of inebriated menfolk became Punkie Night. Whichever version you choose to believe, the modern-day procession mimics this historic trail of lights. In earlier times, once the lanterns had been finished with, farmers would place the Punkies on their gates to ward off evil spirits.

In the current event at Hinton St George, children, many accompanied by their parents, gather at the village hall at around 6.30 p.m. Normally a Punkie King and Queen lead the procession, together with the head man, who wears a white coat and top hat. During the procession the head man rings a bell while those gathered repeatedly sing the Punkie song.

Many of the children dress up in spooky costumes, aligning this oddity more and more with its American cousin. Collections for charity are made along the way from any villagers who open their doors, while some now also offer the children sweets, again echoing the trick or treat aspect of Halloween. Apparently at one time, candles were the desired reward.

After the procession everybody returns to the village hall for refreshments. These might include Punkie-themed biscuits for the young and mulled cider for the adults. The Punkies themselves are judged and prizes given for the best. Traditionally, mangel-wurzels would be cut out to represent a range of scary faces, although many other intricate designs are now also crafted. A good Punkie would have its middle scooped out to leave a very thin layer of orange skin, which really helps to project the glow of the flame inside.

Punkie Night was not unique to Hinton St George; it was once celebrated all over the Somerset Levels and even on the Brendon Hills. Today, you will find further examples at another small village near Crewkerne called Lopen, and at Long Sutton near Langport. There is even a celebration at Chiselborough itself, although here there is no parade, just an indoor Jack o'lantern competition for the children. And high in the Blackdown Hills, a procession now takes place around the Castle Neroche Forset on a Saturday in October.

Because of the similarities, it is possible that the American tradition of Halloween is descended from Punkie Night, although some suggest it might actually be the other way around. Having grown up in Somerset myself, I was certainly aware of Punkie Night long before I had ever heard of Halloween. I can remember this annual parade as a small boy in the 1960s, when, in rural Somerset, nothing like the Halloween celebrations we know today every 31 October had been seen much before the mid-1970s.

Whichever did come first, there is no doubting that the American form of Halloween, since exported back to us, evolved from one, or perhaps several ancient European customs. First there was All Saints' Day, celebrated on 1 November, and All Souls' Day on 2 November, when the spirits of the departed were thought to have been particularly active. Another name for All Saints' Day was All Hallows' Day, and the word Halloween almost certainly derived from the festival being held on the night before All Hallows' Day, or in other words

'All Hallows' Eve'. At the same time of year the Celts held the pagan festival of Samhain, which marked the beginning of winter. There is no evidence that connects this to ghostly activities, although, having said that, the Celts generally believed that evil spirits were decidedly more active during the long nights of winter than during the summer. We can also clearly see a connection with the mumming plays observed earlier, where groups went from house to house hoping to secure food and drink, and similar to trick or treat, would threaten to do mischief if their demands were not met. In fact, here in England one of these occasions was normally held on 4 November and was actually known as Mischief Night. So, there is a colourful mixture of older customs that could lay some claim to being the influence behind what has become a very popular date in the modern calendar.

Visitors to West Witton near Leyburn in North Yorkshire's Wensleydale towards the end of August, may encounter a strange custom known as the Burning of Old Bartle, during which a life-sized effigy of a human figure will be paraded along the main village street accompanied by a crowd led by an appointed 'chanter' who repeatedly chants the Bartle doggerel, as follows:

> On Penhill Crags he tore his rags
> Hunters Thorn he blew his horn
> Cappelbank Stee happened a misfortune and brak' his knee
> Grassgill Beck he brak' his neck
> Wadham's End he couldn't fend,
> Grassgill End we'll mak' his end!
> Shout lads, shout!

This annual ritual begins promptly at 9 p.m. on the Saturday nearest to St Bartholomew's Day, which is celebrated on 24 August. When Old Bartle does eventually arrive at Grassgill End as prophesied in the rhyme, he is ceremonially set alight to the accompaniment of cheers and song.

The Burning of Old Bartle is part of a communal weekend known as the Witton Feast, which really kicks off with a Cottage Show on the Saturday morning and the Witton Fell Race at 6 p.m. that evening. This is a 6.5km (4.1 miles) dash around the Dales: the junior event is 5.9km (3.7 miles). These festivities conclude with a packed programme on the Sunday which is called 'Fun Day' and includes children's sports, fancy dress, falconry, and much more besides.

Bartle himself is made out of old clothes stuffed with straw. He is given a gruesome mask which has small lamps in the eye sockets, to give them an eerie glow. His hair and beard are made from the fleece of a sheep.

*The Burning of Old Bartle,
at West Witton in North
Yorkshire. (Courtesy of Jack
Gritton, www.burningbartle.
org.uk)*

At 9 p.m. the gathered crowd raise a cheer before moving off along the street carrying Bartle to various pubs and houses. At each stop refreshments are taken and the doggerel is chanted again. The procession mindfully stops at the homes of senior citizens, enabling them to come to their windows or doors to see Bartle and enjoy the occasion for themselves. After almost an hour the procession reaches the eastern end of the village, where Bartle is propped up against a drystone wall at the end of Grassgill Lane. Here there is time for one more rendition of the rhyme before the seated effigy is set alight and devoured by flames.

As Old Bartle slowly smoulders into a pile of glowing ashes, the crowd remain a while in contemplation before joining in a round of songs celebrating life in the Yorkshire Dales. Eventually they make their way home or to a local pub for a celebratory drink, proud that they had helped to uphold the tradition for another year.

There are many theories among the Bartle faithful as to who or what Bartle was, and indeed when the custom began. One version dates the tradition to the time of the Protestant Reformation in the sixteenth century, when agents of King Henry VIII sought to confiscate any religious paraphernalia they deemed to be ungodly or even blasphemous. At West Witton, the Church of St Bartholomew is said to have housed a wooden statue of the saint in whose name the building was dedicated. In order for it not to be seized by the reformists, the villagers hid it at several locations before finally losing it at Grassgill. Bartle is thought to have been a derivation of Bartholomew.

Another version claims Bartle was the Abbot Adam Sedburgh (Sedbar) of the nearby Cistercian Jervaulx Abbey, who allegedly tried to avoid taking part in the 'Pilgrimage of Grace'. This was a popular rising in York in 1536 protesting against the Reformation and the Dissolution of the Monasteries. In actual fact, the abbot was very active in the uprising and for his part he was arrested and imprisoned in the Tower of London, where his inscription can be found carved into the wall of his cell: 'Adam Sedbar 1537'. He was one of several abbots put to death, along with thirty-eight monks and sixteen parish priests.

Yet another version claims Bartle was a sheep thief who the villagers chased, caught and burnt at the stake, dealing out their own rough justice after being incensed by his stealing. A further account claims him to have been a giant who was the mortal son of the Viking god Thor. For some unexplained reason he had taken up pig-farming in the area around West Witton. One day, he discovered that his prized boar was missing and blamed the villagers. A feud erupted, which resulted in the locals laying siege to the giant's castle, burning it to the ground, and killing its occupant. Other people inevitably suggest the custom is a descendant form of a pagan harvest ritual. These are just a few of Bartle's possible origins.

In 2005, the Bartle Trail was created to provide a way-marked route of the character's progress around and above the village, in accordance with the doggerel. The 4-mile hike is punctuated by a series of mosaics embedded in stone walls that were crafted by local children and adults. The trail takes you onto the slopes of Penhill where Bartle 'tore his rags', and from where there are splendid vistas across Wensleydale.

Another type of fire is cannon fire: cue the Fenny Poppers. These are six ceremonial cannons fired at Fenny Stratford in Buckinghamshire each St Martin's Day, 11 November, which of course is also the anniversary of Remembrance Day. However, although the custom of firing these pint-sized artillery pieces may appear to be a remembrance salute to the uninitiated, this is completely coincidental. Fenny Stratford, although once an independent rural town, is now an urban district of Milton Keynes, together with Bletchley.

The history of the custom is said to begin with a gentleman named Browne Willis, who was the Member of Parliament for Buckingham between 1705 and 1708, and an obsessive antiquarian. Willis had inherited the manor of Water Eaton with Fenny Stratford and Bletchley in 1700 and lived at Whaddon Hall. He was the grandson of a notable physician of his time, Dr Thomas Willis, in whose memory he had erected St Martin's Church at Fenny Stratford on the site of the old Chantry Chapel of St Margaret and St Catherine. This was partly because his grandfather, who was a resident of St Martin's Lane in the parish of St Martin-in-the-Fields, died on St Martin's Day in 1675. Browne Willis had bought the site in 1724 using funds he had raised himself to provide a new church for local residents, which was completed in 1730.

During his own lifetime, Willis also celebrated the occasion with an annual dinner to which members of the local gentry and clergy were invited. Following his death, and in order to perpetuate his own memory, he left arrangements for a sermon to be preached at St Martin's Church each St Martin's Day, for which a fee was payable.

Although there are no records of their inaugural firing, the Fenny Poppers are said to date from this time and are claimed to have been presented to the town by Browne Willis himself. The six poppers are tankard shaped and are cast from gun metal, each weighing 19lbs (8.6 kg). They have a bore of 1.75ins x 6ins (150mm x 45mm), and are loaded with a charge of Pyrodex, which is a modern substitute for gunpowder ,which was originally used. After being plugged with newspaper rammed down the barrel, they are detonated with a long firing rod, which is held to an aperture along their sides.

In order to pay for both the gunpowder and the annual sermon, Willis purchased a house in Aylesbury Street, Fenny Stratford, and used the rent it generated. After his death both traditions were maintained and the Fenny Poppers were fired every year from a paddock near the Bull and Butcher Inn. However, after one of them exploded in 1856, damaging the roof of the pub, it was decided that new canons were needed.

This is the official story, but as with all customs there are disagreeing minds when it comes to the origins of the poppers. Some years ago, Michael Brace researched a booklet on the history of the poppers and he concluded that the day as celebrated by Browne Willis merely involved the sermon and the dinner paid for by the rent from the house in Aylesbury Street. He is convinced that the poppers were introduced at a later date and not by Browne Willis at all. He is also sure that it was his grandfather and not himself that he wished to be remembered.

The six Poppers that are still used today were forged in 1859 at the Eagle Foundry in Northampton. They are believed to have been made using one

The Fenny Poppers being fired at Fenny Stratford on St Martin's Day. The heated end of a long rod is brought into contact with the touch-hole. (Courtesy of Michael Brace)

This photograph gives a good idea of the size and shape of a Fenny Popper. (Courtesy of Michael Brace)

of the originals as a pattern, but as none of these exist, their exact shape is not known.

The current location for firing the battery is the Leon Recreation Ground. This land once belonged to the Chantry. From here they are fired three times on St Martin's Day: 12 noon, 2 p.m. and 4 p.m. Previously they are known to have been fired from several other locations, including the Grand Union Canal Wharf, land behind the church, St Martin's Hall, and the churchyard itself.

Over the centuries the poppers have also been fired to mark other great national events, such as the death of Queen Victoria in 1901; the start of the new Millennium on 1 January 2000; and the 100th birthday of the Queen Mother on 4 August 2000. Today, they also lend their name to the annual Fenny Poppers Festival in August. This is a street festival when Aylesbury Street in Fenny Stratford is closed to traffic. During the festival just one Fenny Popper is fired on the day – at 2 p.m. by the vicar.

17

BONFIRE NIGHT

THE EVENT WHICH has given rise to more fire-related celebrations than any other was the Gunpowder Plot of 1605. Villages and towns all around the country still light bonfires on 5 November in remembrance of this occasion, as they have done for hundreds of years, while others hold lavish firework displays.

Bonfire Night is enjoyed in a wide variety of ways, ranging from large civic demonstrations to small family garden parties where fireworks are lit to the delight of children, while hot dogs, beef burgers, and flasks of soup or cocoa protect them from the chilly night air. This makes Bonfire Night one of the most popular and well-supported customs of all, with fireworks such as rockets, bangers and Catherine Wheels part of everyday language and the name Guy Fawkes renowned as one of history's greatest villains. But why, over 400 years later, do we still 'remember, remember, the fifth of November?'

During the reign of Queen Elizabeth I, Catholics had been persecuted in England. The Queen was a Protestant and similar to her father before her, King Henry VIII, she was the head of the Church of England. In fact, Henry had initially been a Catholic himself, but when the Pope refused to grant him a divorce from his first wife, Catherine of Aragon, he broke with Rome and declared himself supreme head of the Church of England.

When Elizabeth died, King James I succeeded her to the throne. James was already King of Scotland, a country that largely remained faithful to Catholicism. Even the King's mother openly practised the older faith. This gave Catholics in England rise to believe that they would once again be tolerated. However, James proved to be little more tolerant than his predecessor. Incensed by this, a group of young

Catholic activists, led by a man called Sir Robert Catesby, decided that violent action was the only course open to them, so they hatched a plot to blow up Parliament and kill the King and the Prince of Wales.

The conspirators planned to execute their scheme during the annual State Opening of Parliament in November 1605, when the King was certain to be in attendance. In May 1604, they rented a house next to the Palace of Westminster where Parliament met and proceeded to dig a tunnel through to a cellar underneath the House of Lords. Here they stored thirty-six barrels of gunpowder. As the plan began to take shape it seems that one of the conspirators had second thoughts. Innocent people would inevitably be killed or injured in the attack and, as well as politicians who opposed Catholicism, there were representatives in the House who had actively supported it. If any of these were killed, it would probably do their cause more harm than good.

One of the group is said to have sent an anonymous letter to Lord Monteagle, deploring him to stay away from Parliament on 5 November. In due course the letter came to the attention of the King and a search of the area led to the discovery of one of the terrorists concealed in the cellar among the barrels of gunpowder. Guido (Guy) Fawkes was caught red-handed.

Fawkes was arrested and put in the Tower of London, where he was tortured for several months. The King himself signed the warrant permitting his cruel ordeal. Finally, along with the other conspirators, he was hanged, drawn and quartered.

Today, the reigning monarch only enters Parliament once a year, on what is still called the State Opening of Parliament. Prior to their arrival the Yeomen of the Guard search the cellars. However, the existing Houses of Parliament are very different from those which the plotters had tried to bomb. Much of the Palace of Westminster was destroyed by a fire in October 1834 and rebuilt between 1840 and 1870.

On the very night that the Gunpowder Plot was foiled, 5 November 1605, bonfires were set alight to joyfully celebrate the deliverance of the King from mortal danger, and the tradition has continued from that day to this. In 1606, an Act of Parliament established a public 'Thanksgiving to Almighty God every year on the 5 November', which required the ringing of the church bells and the conducting of a service in every parish in England. As time passed, people began to place effigies of Guy Fawkes onto their burning pyres, while others even added representations of the Pope himself.

Preparations for Bonfire Night begin several weeks before the event, as people collect wood, cardboard boxes and anything else that will burn, in order to build their bonfires as high as possible. Children often make a dummy of

Guy Fawkes, which is universally called 'the Guy'. In the days leading up to the celebration, this dummy will either be propped up against a wall in a public place, or paraded through the streets in a wheelbarrow. The children in charge of it will beg those who pass for 'a penny for the Guy'. This money is then used to purchase fireworks for the evening festivities, although today most of them are resigned to the fact that they will have to enjoy the organised displays put on by local clubs. On Bonfire Night itself the Guy is placed on top of the bonfire, which is then set alight. The firework displays usually follow.

Bonfire Night celebrations vary from place to place and among the most spectacular are those held in the town of Lewes in Sussex, which tens of thousands of people attend each year. These particular celebrations are noted for their anarchical devil-may-care attitude towards authority, religion, political correctness and, sometimes, even health and safety. Although culminating with a series of bonfires, the occasion features torch-lit processions through the town organised by clubs known as bonfire societies under the auspices of Lewes Bonfire Council. However, these celebrations have a chequered history of unruliness.

Smugglers of the Commercial Square Bonfire Society taking part in the Lewes Bonfire celebrations. (Courtesy of Peter Trimming)

Although bonfires were undoubtedly burned in Lewes during the years that followed the Gunpowder Plot, the first indication that future celebrations here would be more notable than those in other places came in 1679, when a Pope-burning procession was held through the borough. The first recorded bonfire is mentioned in the diary of John Holman, the High Constable of Lewes in 1813, as taking place on Gallows Bank. The custom of dragging blazing tar barrels through the streets was introduced in 1829. Over the next few years local magistrates attempted to stop these dangerous practices from taking place, but the bonfire boys, as they were known, displayed even greater energy in response.

On 5 November 1838, rioting took place in the town when a magistrate, Mr Whitfield JP, had a sharp encounter with the boys on Cliffe Bridge. Several arrests were made and fines of up to £15 were imposed. But more trouble was to follow. In 1841, special constables were sworn in to help stop the celebrations. On this occasion the bonfire boys armed themselves, which unfortunately led to more than twenty rioters being sent to prison for up to two months each. Another attempt to clear the boys from the streets was made in 1846, which led to more rioting and another magistrate, Mr Blackman JP, being seriously injured.

In 1847, 170 of the town's principal tradesmen and other respectable citizens were summoned to be sworn in as special constables. On their way to a meeting on 5 November they were attacked by bonfire boys in the High Street. Tar barrels were lit and running battles occurred with the police, who formed a chain across Keere Street, which resulted in several arrests. The next day, the Metropolitan Constabulary sent a hundred officers to the town as more trouble was expected. Things came to a head when Lord Chichester read the Riot Act on the steps of County Hall and gave the crowd five minutes to disperse. In the free fight that ensued many of the Metropolitan Police officers were injured, although the streets were eventually cleared. This was the final serious disorder to happen during the history of the Lewes Bonfire Night celebrations, since when things have been decidedly more convivial.

Today there are seven bonfire societies, called Cliffe, Commercial Square, Lewes Borough, South Street, Waterloo, Southover and Nevill Juvenile. The Cliffe Society, founded in 1853, has the reputation of being the most controversial in terms of political correctness. They also reputedly field the loudest fireworks. Of the others, Waterloo is perhaps the most family-orientated, while Nevill Juvenile, as its name suggests, is run for children. Each of these societies proceeds through the town on separate routes, often accompanied by the representatives of other societies from neighbouring towns, although occasionally their paths collide.

These celebrations, with the exception of those held by the Nevill Juvenile Society, always take place on 5 November, unless the night falls on a Sunday, in which case they will be held on the 4th. Those of the Nevill Juvenile Society are always held a couple of weeks earlier at the Nevill Estate, with the bonfire and fireworks display on the nearby South Downs.

Each society has its own motto, emblem and traditional costumes, which include the outfits of Mongol warriors and Cavaliers. The motto of the Lewes Borough Bonfire Society, for instance, is 'Death or Glory'. Their members parade in one of three different guises, with their main outfit being that of a smuggler. Others might be dressed as Zulu warriors or Tudor folk, which in bonfire talk are categorised as their first and second pioneers. Sian Riddle, secretary of the society, provides the following explanation:

> The smuggler outfit was the first one worn by the society in 1853. The boys wore royal blue and white striped jerseys, red hats and wore face masks so they could not be identified easily. This was because the authorities were not in favour of the celebrations. We now also wear red sashes and no longer hide our faces. The smugglers are a large part of the society and it is this uniform that is usually worn when members are working on the night. This includes marshalling, carrying the tar barrel, distributing torches and carrying the banners and set pieces.
>
> Zulus are Ye Olde Lewes Borough Bonfire Society's first pioneers. They appeared in 1948 with Mexicans but in 1949 they became the only first pioneers. Over the years the head dresses have become bigger and brighter some reaching nine feet tall. During the 1950s, Ted Over used to bring some young people dressed in grass skirts, beads and fuzzy black hair from Brighton to join the ranks of the Zulus. This of course does not happen now. The outfits are all homemade including the head dresses and beading, which takes many hours of hard work.
>
> Tudors are Ye Olde Lewes Borough Bonfire Society's second pioneers. It is not clear when the Tudor dress became the second pioneer but we know it has been since the 1950s. These costumes are again homemade and take a lot of hard work, especially all the decoration that is put on them.

Each 5 November the first parade of the evening is to the war memorial. All the societies have set pieces of poppies and 'Lest We Forget' banners which are lit up, commemorating all those who have died and been injured in conflicts right up to the present day. The 'Last Post' is played followed by a minute's silence and then 'Reveille'. The parade to the cenotaph is walked at a slow pace, with a slightly quicker step on the return.

Tudor ladies burn torches at the Lewes Bonfire. (Courtesy of Lewes Borough Bonfire Society)

Lewes Borough carry four burning crosses at the remembrance service, which are said to commemorate the memory of Protestant martyrs who were burnt at the stake in the town during the period known as the Marian Persecutions. This reference relates to the persecution of religious reformers for their beliefs during the reign of Queen Mary I of England (1553-1558), which earned her the nickname 'Bloody Mary'. This was probably a little unfair as the atrocities were more likely carried out by other people in her name, rather than with her full knowledge.

During the celebrations a number of large effigies are also drawn through the streets, with Guy Fawkes and Pope Paul V, who was head of the Roman Catholic Church in 1605, appearing without fail. Nationally reviled figures topical at the time are represented. Other features of these parades might include burning upside-down crosses, or chanting 'Burn the Pope'. The Cliffe Society controversially displays the effigied heads on pikes of people they regard as the enemies of bonfire. These again range from nationally reviled figures to local officials who have attempted to place restrictions on the event, whose efforts are largely treated with contempt by the societies. The effigies are finally destroyed by the flames of one of the culminating bonfires.

During their final procession the Lewes Borough Bonfire Society carry a key known as the 'Monster iron key of the ancient Borough of Lewes' which, at

Tudor lady of the Lewes Borough Bonfire Society holding a burning cross before the war memorial. These crosses represent Protestant martyrs who were burnt at the stake in the town during the Marian Persecutions. (Courtesy of Lewes Borough Bonfire Society)

other times of the year can be seen on display at Anne of Cleves House, Lewes. This key, which weighs nearly a quarter of a hundredweight, is carried as a symbol that on Bonfire Night alone, the bonfire boys and girls of the society are given the freedom of the town, being the only one of the seven societies to be granted such an honour.

Another aspect of the festival is the throwing of a flaming tar barrel into the River Ouse, which is said to symbolise the throwing into the river of magistrates after they had read the Riot Act to the bonfire boys during one of the nineteenth-century riots. But again, as with many traditions, this may echo earlier Samhain lore, when at the start of November the Celts marked the beginning of winter.

The history of the Lewes Bonfire has had many ups and downs, with one of its most memorable years being 2005, when, to celebrate the 400th anniversary of the Gunpowder Plot, there was a fantastic display of costumes and a record-breaking 40ft Guy.

At Ottery St Mary in Devon, burning tar barrels are the focus of another spectacular event held on 5 November each year that might also trace its origins back to the Gunpowder Plot. As we have already observed through Golowan, the West Country has a history of torch-lit processions and a habit for burning tar barrels. In most instances, these were traditionally rolled through the streets, which itself seems quite a dangerous pastime. But at Ottery St Mary, at some twist in the town's hazy past, someone decided that it would be a better idea to carry the burning cooperage on their shoulders instead. The result is one of the country's most dramatic and heart-stopping rituals. Although the custom was not unique to this Devonshire backwater, today it remains the only place where full-sized lighted tar barrels are borne in this way. The ceremony always happens on the 5th, unless it falls on a Sunday, in which case the antics occur on the day before.

Naturally, there are those who distance the festival from the events of 1605 and other suggestions as to its origin include the theory that it dates from 1588, when beacons were built around the country and set alight as a warning that the Spanish Armada had been sighted in the Channel. Others claim that it relates to the ancient practice of fumigating cottages, or a Pagan belief that fire cleansed the streets of evil spirits.

Each year seventeen barrels are carefully selected and lined with a coating of coal tar, all of which can take several months to prepare. The barrels are then slotted into one of three categories. Not all of them are going to be carried by big, burly, men, as even boys, girls and women participate. 'Small' barrels are reserved for boys and girls, 'medium' for women and youths, while the men take on the 'gert big unz' which can weigh at least 30 kilos.

Sandhill Street in Ottery St Mary is lit up by a burning tar barrel. (Photo courtesy of Lewis Clarke)

The proceedings start in the afternoon with the children's and women's barrels, which need to get off to a cracking start. They have to stick to a tight schedule in order to finish in the town square at around midnight, bearing in mind that during the evening the barrels have become progressively larger.

Each barrel, packed full of paper and straw, is first set alight. Within seconds it erupts into a billowing funnel of flames as the contents ignite and the melting tar begins to do its work. It is then hoisted onto the shoulders of the 'barrel roller' and as they move forward, clutching their load with fire-resistant gauntlets, the gathered crowd can feel the lick of its intense heat. Before long the barrel itself begins to burn and quite literally fall apart at the seams, stave by stave. Flames christen each barrel outside one of the town's numerous pubs or hotels, where strong ales or cider no doubt help to steady the nerves. As a spectator sport, it is certainly not one for the faint-hearted.

Over the centuries, successive generations of the same families have proudly carried barrels on 5 November. They have willingly faced the prospect of sustaining serious injury in a bid to perpetuate the tradition, for in truth, they get little else out of it. Today, the safety of the rollers is of course of paramount concern, but injuries do occur.

Although visitors are welcome to watch from the sidelines, the festival is first and foremost for the people of Ottery St Mary itself. Onlookers who flock to the event in their tens of thousands are often regarded as a hindrance, as they congest the narrow streets and make life difficult for those carrying the barrels. They also have a reputation of drinking to excess and causing a noisy distraction, at a time when concentration is critical. These visitors can only really appreciate what they are seeing from the surface, which is an exciting festival of fire. For locals, who are more in tune with the history of the tradition, there is a great sense of inherent pride, particularly if a fledgling member of their own fold is participating for their first time. Of course as village communities, particularly in the West Country, become more and more diluted by outside influences, customs like this are certain to lose some of their sociological significance.

To coincide with the festival, the people of Ottery also contribute towards the building of the town's great bonfire, which is sited at a place called St Saviour's Meadow. Anything that will burn is eagerly gathered in and hauled to the site in a fully-laden trailer, pulled by a tractor. By the eve of Bonfire Night the fruit of their labour towers to roughly 35ft and has a girth of around 50ft. Since 1958, the Guy has been provided by members of the same family, the Youngs. On festival day he is placed on top of the bonfire and during the evening, as the streets echo to the fervour of tar barrel burning and the traditional funfair, the Carnival Vice President puts a flaming torch to the base of the stack, to the delight of all present. Carnival processions are another important West Country tradition associated with the Gunpowder Plot, which are covered in the following chapter. The example at Ottery St Mary is usually held on the Saturday prior to the Tar Barrels.

18

GUY FAWKES
CARNIVALS

THE STANDARD WEST Country carnival is a parade of illuminated floats or 'carts', so-called because they were originally constructed from hay or log carts. There are a number of circuits, the best-known and biggest of which are probably the Guy Fawkes Carnivals of Somerset, with the town of Bridgwater regarded as the 'home of carnival'. The annual celebrations here were first held on 5 November and without question date back many centuries. However, there are no records of the early years as newspapers did not appear in the town until the mid-nineteenth century, which leaves researchers with only tantalising threads of information to go on.

The carnival's official website suggests that the deaths of one John Taylor and his two children recorded in the parish records of St Mary's Church in 1716 were linked to that year's event. Their demise was due to a gunpowder explosion in their home during the tell-tale month of November. A possible explanation for this being that they were making 'squibs', a term coined in the town for hand-made fireworks. The squibs were held aloft on the end of long wooden poles called coshes. These were uniquely made around the Somerset town and originally known as 'Bridgwater Squibs'. At one time they would extinguish with a loud bang, but with modern health and safety regulations, and insurance concerns, the bang has long since been abolished. As early as 1892 the Home Office showed concern about the dangers of people making fireworks in their own homes, so today the squibs are only produced by reputed manufacturers using a secret formula. On modern carnival nights over a hundred 'squibbers' line the town's High Street, making a colourful display.

The squibbing display after the Bridgwater Carnival procession makes a spectacular sight. (Courtesy of Phil Williams)

The original celebrations in Bridgwater consisted of a large bonfire built at the Cornhill, which was right in the centre of the town. Being a port and located at a point where the River Parrett meets the Bristol Channel, a large discarded boat would be used each year as the base. This would be stuffed with a hundred tar barrels and anything else available to burn.

Gangs of young men would throw Guys on the fire, which were representations of the gunpowder plotters. These effigies would be paraded towards the inferno and it was from these humble beginnings that the annual procession was born. Year by year the tradition strengthened, with music, dance and costume eventually being added. By the 1880s, elaborate outfits were already a major feature of the festivities; even spectators are known to have worn masks, which in a way enabled a certain amount of mischief-making.

But why was Bridgwater so profoundly affected by the gunpowder plot? It was probably due to the fact that most of the townsfolk were staunchly Protestant at the time, while one of the alleged masterminds behind the scheme, Robert Parsons, was a Catholic priest from the nearby village of Nether Stowey. This coincidence no doubt fuelled seething towards this local traitor, while at the same time rejoicing at the failure of his plan.

The celebrations of 1880 were marred by drunken disorder which by the early hours of the morning had manifested into a full-blown riot, with a crowd of some 300 people still partying around the bonfire and rival gangs squaring up to each other. The local authority decided, in their wisdom, that the best way to disperse the crowd was for the fire brigade to douse the flames. This proved to be a big mistake as it further enraged the troublemakers, who turned the hoses onto the firemen themselves, while cutting through others. One brigade member, James Ware, was set upon as he tried to defend a standpipe. He managed to escape home but was forced to remain inside under police protection.

It was as a result of this unacceptable behaviour that the modern carnival came about, as in the following year, 1881, the first carnival committee was formed, largely due to the efforts of a gentleman called Frank Squire. The committee established the event as a procession, so that people could enjoy the spectacle in different parts of the town. By keeping the gangs moving it also meant there was less chance of further drunken violence. That year the first official Bridgwater Guy Fawkes Carnival took place, making it the country's longest-running event. It has taken place every year since that time, except during the two world wars. However, to keep the tradition's unbroken lineage intact during the Second World War, a group called the Kilties, led by a certain William Lockyer, walked the route each year.

The bonfire at the Cornhill was finally abandoned in 1925, after the area on which it was traditionally built was laid with tarmacadam, to accommodate the growth of motor transport in the town. This now left the carnival procession as the sole focus of attention.

There were a number of other landmark dates in the carnival's history. In 1883, for instance, when a new town bridge was built over the River Parrett, it was decided to open it officially on the afternoon of the carnival. That evening, as the procession crossed the new bridge for the inaugural time, it was greeted by a spectacular firework display, which the committee had funded by holding a concert at the Town Hall, which raised fourteen guineas. Similar to the carnival itself, concerts have been staged every year ever since, except during the war years, and they remain an important source of funding for this annual fiesta. At these concerts members of the various carnival clubs perform on stage wearing costumes and using scenery taken from their carts, thus providing the audience with a flavour of what to expect in the approaching series of town parades.

One of the defining characteristics of a carnival float today is the intensity of light and heat generated by tens of thousands of light bulbs. In earlier times the entries were illuminated by paraffin lamps carried alongside. The first electric lights appeared on an entry in 1903. It goes without saying that these earlier carts were pulled by horses. Today they are towed by tractors and the last entry pulled by horse-power was recorded in 1948.

Until 1909, the parade was held on bonfire night itself, but in that year it was decided to hold future events on the Thursday nearest 5 November, the reason for this being that Thursday was the town's early closing day. Today Bridgwater Carnival is held on the Friday nearest Guy Fawkes Night and has been since 2001. This decision was taken in order to maintain its position as the country's premier carnival, as the Thursday slot was seen as restrictive for many spectators. Also, Glastonbury Carnival, which is held on a Saturday, was beginning to steal Bridgwater's thunder by earning itself the reputation of being the best show in the West. From 2012, Bridgwater Carnival will itself be moving to the first Saturday in November for a three-year trial.

Over the years many more West Country towns have established their own carnivals, which are grouped together in local circuits. This enables the clubs to parade their carts at a number of different venues. Bridgwater Carnival is now the opening show of the Somerset County Guy Fawkes Carnival Association Circuit and is followed by events at North Petherton; Highbridge and Burnham-on-Sea; Shepton Mallet; Wells; Glastonbury and Chilkwell; and Weston-super-Mare. There is also an unofficial procession at Midsomer Norton.

Other circuits include the Wessex Grand Prix Circuit; the South Somerset Federation of Carnivals Circuit; the South Devon Carnival Circuit; and the East Devon Carnival Circuit. But this type of carnival is certainly no longer a preserve of the West Country and similar events can now be observed across the country. Whether or not their inspiration is drawn from the Gunpowder Plot of 1605 is another matter.

Some of these processions can include as many as sixty carts, which carnival club members build throughout the year. The carts are basically long trailers pulled behind tractors, built up with elaborate scenery illustrating a chosen theme such as space travel, pirates, or a children's book. Club members will also wear costumes that complement the theme and ride on the cart either dancing in unison to loud music or standing perfectly still, which is known as 'in tableau format'. The tractors also tow large diesel-driven electricity generators, which provide the power for the light bulbs that illuminate the scenes, often numbering in excess of 20,000. These carts are very expensive to put together and are funded by charitable donations, sponsorship from local businesses, or by putting on fund-raising initiatives like a disco or jumble sale.

The clubs themselves are normally raised through working or social networks. These might be local industries, groups such as the Young Farmers,

'Egyptian Blue', an entry from Gorgons Carnival Club at the Bridgwater Guy Fawkes Carnival. (Courtesy of Shelly Ford, Gorgons Carnival Club)

or even a public house. There are dozens of them with names like Gremlins, Griffens, and Masqueraders.

During actual processions the carts, which take roughly two hours to complete an average route, will be interspersed with walking exhibits, troupes of majorettes, or marching bands. To add excitement and competition, trophies will be awarded to the best entries. There will also be money-collecting carts and people in costumes walking along with collection buckets. The crowds, which at Bridgwater regularly exceed 100,000, are encouraged to give generously and all the money raised on the night is donated to local charities.

West Country carnivals today are as popular as ever, with people coming from all over the country to spectate. In 2005, a statue was unveiled on the Cornhill in Bridgwater called 'The Spirit of Carnival' to mark the spot where, 400 years before, a West Country tradition was born.

The year 2012 marks a new chapter in the history of Bridgwater Carnival, when the parade moves to a Saturday for the first time in over 100 years. The organisers will be taking this opportunity to encourage more people from the local community to take part in the annual celebrations. Pupils at local schools will be invited to design and make models of carnival carts as well as participate in making carnival craft items. On carnival day itself, there will also be a children's parade in the afternoon.

The week before the carnival local groups will be invited to stage their own productions, which will be publicised under the carnival 'umbrella' but which will also help those concerned to raise funds and entertain the public in their own way.

Throughout the year there will be opportunities to learn new carnival skills through a series of workshops at the local Bridgwater College. And with the Olympics in mind, 100 squibbers will be taking part in the opening ceremonies to be staged at Weymouth and Portland.

In October 2010, the Bridgwater Carnival Centre opened its doors for the very first time. Located in the town's High Street, right next door to the Town Hall, the centre provides visitors with information about the town's most famous event, offers a range of souvenirs whose sales help boost the carnival coffers, and houses a display of carnival memorabilia. So, after 130 years of organised carnivals, Bridgwater Carnival now has a home of its own in the 'Home of Carnival'.

FEATURED CUSTOMS

This list is based on previous years, so please check for current status and dates before attending any of these events.

Arbor Day: Aston-on-Clun, Shropshire – Last Sunday in May

Ball Game: Atherstone, Warwickshire – Shrove Tuesday

Ball Game: Sedgefield, Co. Durham – Shrove Tuesday

Bawming the Thorn: Appleton Thorn, Cheshire – Third Saturday in June

Beating the Bounds: Oxford, Oxon – Ascension Day

Beating the Bounds: Portland, Dorset – Ascension Day every seven years

Beating the Bounds: Tower of London – Ascension Day every three years

Burning of Old Bartle: West Witton, North Yorkshire – 24 August

Burning the Ashen Faggot: Axmouth, Devon – Christmas Eve

Burning the Ashen Faggot: Curry Rivel, Somerset – 5 January

Burning the Ashen Faggot: Shave Cross, Dorset – 17 January

Cheese Rolling: Chester, Cheshire – Easter weekend

Cheese Rolling and Wake: Cooper's Hill, Gloucestershire – Spring bank holiday Monday

Cheese Rolling: Findon, West Sussex – Coronation days

Cheese Rolling: Randwick, Gloucestershire – First Sunday in May

Cheese Rolling: Stilton, Cambridgeshire – May Day bank holiday Monday

Egremont Crab Fair and Sports: Egremont, Cumbria – Third Saturday in September

Fenny Poppers: Fenny Stratford, Buckinghamshire – 11 November

Flitch Trials: Great Dunmow, Essex – A Saturday in July Leap Year's only

Garland Day: Castleton, Derbyshire – 29 May

Golowan Festival: Penzance, Cornwall – Nine days in late June

Gurning World Championships: Egremont, Cumbria – Third Saturday in September

Guy Fawkes Carnival: Bridgwater, Somerset – First Saturday in November

Hare Pie Scramble and Bottle Kicking: Hallaton, Leicestershire – Easter Monday

Haxey Hood Game: Haxey, Lincolnshire – 6 January

Hobby Horse Festival: Banbury, Oxfordshire – First weekend in July

Hobby Horse Festival: Minehead, Somerset – May Day

Hobby Horse Festival: Padstow, Cornwall – May Day

Hocktide: Hungerford, Berkshire – Second Tuesday after Easter

Hunting of the Earl of Rone: Combe Martin, Devon – Spring bank holiday weekend

Hurling the Silver Ball: St Columb Major, Cornwall – Shrove Tuesday

Jack in the Green: Brentham, London – Second Saturday in May

Jack in the Green: Bristol – First Saturday in May

Jack in the Green: Deptford, London – 1 May

Jack in the Green: Guildford, Surrey – Saturday before May Day bank holiday

Jack in the Green: Hastings, East Sussex – May Day bank holiday weekend

Jack in the Green: Ilfracombe, Devon – May Day bank holiday Monday

Jack in the Green: Knutsford, Cheshire – First Saturday in May

Jack in the Green: London – 1 May

Jack in the Green: Oxford, Oxfordshire – 1 May

Jack in the Green: Rochester, Kent – May Day bank holiday weekend

Jack in the Green: Whitstable, Kent – 1 May

Knutsford Royal May Day: Knutsford, Cheshire – First Saturday in May

Lewes Bonfire: Lewes, East Sussex – 5 November

Mumming: Chester, Cheshire – Around All Souls' Day 2 November and St George's Day, 23 April

Oak Apple Day: Great Wishford, Wiltshire – 29 May

Olney Pancake Race: Olney, Buckinghamshire – Shrove Tuesday

Plague Service: Eyam, Derbyshire – Last Sunday in August

Punkie Night: Hinton St George, Somerset – Last Thursday in October

Randwick Wap: Randwick, Gloucestershire – the Saturday following the first Sunday in May

Rochester Sweeps Festival: Rochester, Kent – May Day Weekend

Royal Shrovetide Football Match: Ashbourne, Derbyshire – Shrove Tuesday and Ash Wednesday

Rushbearing: Ambleside, Cumbria – First Saturday in July

Rushbearing: Grasmere, Cumbria – July last Saturday in school's summer term

Rushbearing: Great Musgrave, Cumbria – First Saturday in July

Rushbearing: Littleborough, Greater Manchester – A weekend in July

Rushbearing: Saddleworth Valley, Greater Manchester – Second weekend in August

Rushbearing: Sowerby Bridge, Yorkshire – First weekend in September

Rushbearing: Urswick, Cumbria – Sunday nearest 29 September

Rushbearing: Warcop, Cumbria – 29 June

Scarborough Skipping Festival: Scarborough, North Yorkshire – Shrove Tuesday

Scoring the Hales: Alnwick, Northumberland – Shrove Tuesday

Shrove Tuesday Football Ceremony of the Purbeck Marblers: Corfe Castle, Dorset – Shrove Tuesday

Tar Barrels: Ottery St Mary, Devon – 5 November

Tree Dressing: Weald and Downland Open Air Museum, Singleton, West Sussex – First Sunday in December

Wassailing: Bolney, West Sussex – First Saturday in January

Wassailing: Carhampton, Somerset – 17 January

Wassailing: Firle, East Sussex – Second Saturday in January

Wassailing: Whimple, Devon – 17 January

Well Dressing: Buxton, Derbyshire – A week in July, beginning on the Sunday before the second Wednesday in the month

Well Dressing: Eyam, Derbyshire – Week beginning the Saturday prior to the last Sunday in August

Well Dressing: Tissington, Derbyshire – Ascension Day

Whalton Bale: Whalton, Northumberland – 4 July

Whittlesea Straw Bear Festival: Whittlesey, Cambridgeshire – Second weekend in January

Wilkes Walk: Leighton Buzzard, Bedfordshire – Rogation Monday

If you enjoyed reading this book, you may also be interested in...

Kent Folk Tales

TONY COOPER

These traditional stories and local legends have been handed down by storytellers for centuries. Herein you will find the intriguing tales of Brave Mary of Mill Hill, King Herla, the Pickpockets of Sturry, the Wantsum Wyrm and the Battle of Sandwich, to name but a few. These captivating stories, brought to life with a collection of unique illustrations, will be enjoyed by readers time and again.

978 0 7524 5933 2

Wiltshire Folk Tales

KIRSTY HARTSIOTIS

These lively and entertaining folk tales from one of Britain's most ancient counties are vividly retold by local storyteller Kirsty Hartsiotis. Their origins lost in the oral tradition, these thirty stories from Wiltshire reflect the wisdom of the county and its people. Discover Merlin's trickery, King Alfred's bravery, along with dabchicks and the Devil, the flying monk of Malmesbury and the ravenous maggot of Little Langford. These tales bring alive the landscape of the county's ancient barrows, stone circles and rolling hills.

978 0 7524 5736 9

Shropshire Folk Tales

AMY DOUGLAS

The thirty stories in this new collection have grown out of the county's diverse landscapes: tales of the strange and macabre; memories of magic and other worlds; proud recollections of folk history; stories to make you smile, sigh and shiver. Moulded by the land, weather and generations of tongues wagging, these traditional tales are full of Shropshire wit and wisdom, and will be enjoyed time and again.

978 0 7524 5155 8

Folklore of Lincolnshire

SUSANNA O'NEILL

With one of the most interesting dialects in the country, this vast region is also rich in superstitions, songs and traditional games. A study of the daily life, lore and customs of Lincolnshire are here interspersed with stories of monstrous black hounds, dragon lairs, witches, Tiddy Mun, mischievous imps and tales of the people known as the Yellowbellies. This fully illustrated book explores the origins and meanings of Lincolnshire's traditions and shows how the customs of the past have influenced the ways of the present.

978 0 7524 5964 6

Visit our website and discover thousands of other History Press books.

www.thehistorypress.co.uk